BRITISH AND COMMONWEALTH ACES OF WORLD WAR II

BRITISH AND COMMONWEALTH ACES OF WORLD WAR II

THE PICTORIAL RECORD

Norman Franks

Schiffer Military History
Atglen, PA

Book design by Robert Biondi.

Library of Congress Catalog Number: 2006928352.

Printed in China.
ISBN: 0-7643-2525-6

Published by Schiffer Publishing Ltd.
4880 Lower Valley Road
Atglen, PA 19310
Phone: (610) 593-1777
FAX: (610) 593-2002
E-mail: Info@schifferbooks.com.
Visit our web site at: www.schifferbooks.com
Please write for a free catalog.
This book may be purchased from the publisher.
Please include $3.95 postage.
Try your bookstore first.

In Europe, Schiffer books are distributed by:
Bushwood Books
6 Marksbury Ave.
Kew Gardens, Surrey TW9 4JF
England
Phone: 44 (0)20 8392-8585
FAX: 44 (0)20 8392-9876
E-mail: info@bushwoodbooks.co.uk
www.bushwoodbooks.co.uk
Free postage in the UK. Europe: air mail at cost.
Try your bookstore first.

INTRODUCTION

While there have been a number of books on World War II fighter aces since the end of that conflict, there has not been one covering just the photographic record of these men. Because of the total number involved I have had to limit the scope to just those who scored, or were credited with, ten or more victories.

In order to do this sensibly I have to start by getting on my 'hobby-horse' when it comes to victory totals. I have never understood the predilection of those who need to add shares and fractions of claims together in order to reach a final number. To my mind a fighter pilot on his own destroys an enemy aircraft, and if he assists in the destruction of others, there is no sense in adding fractions such as 33%, 25%, 50%, or the even more ridiculous 16%, then coming up with some weird total.

With this method, a pilot who, say, claims seven victories on his own, has half shares in four more, a third share in another, and a 6th share in yet another, will be shown as having 9.49 victories. Looking at this figure quickly it appears to be a simple 9 1/2, but realistically it is seven and six shares. Therefore this pilot has destroyed or helped to destroy thirteen enemy machines. Anyway, that's how I see it and that is how I have selected the pilots with ten or more victories – on their own or shared – to be included in this book.

Where possible I have used photographs of night fighter pilots with their Navigator/Radar Operator, these men sharing their victories as a team. In a few instances a pilot's radar operator is shown in a separate photo but next to the one of his pilot.

I have, of course, relied heavily on the book *Aces High* by my good friend Chris Shores, who I have known and had a close relationship with for forty years. His research is virtually beyond question and he has been a dedicated historian for longer than I have known him. He and I worked on *Above the Trenches*, a similar book to his *Aces High*, but dealing with the British and Commonwealth aces of the Great War.

The object, of course, with this book, is to have a volume of portraits of these ace pilots 'under one roof'. It is in similar vein to two earlier Schiffer publications: *German Aces of World War I*, that Greg VanWyngarden and I produced in 2004; and *British and American Aces of World War I,* that I did myself in 2005.

The photo captions should be self-explanatory. Name and rank, birth and death dates where known, decorations and awards, squadrons and units served with while operational, their victory totals, and the theatres of operations in which they flew. All the aces depicted flew at some stage with the Royal Air Force, or under its umbrella, so that it covers Canadians, Australians, New Zealanders, Americans, South Africans, Norwegians, French, Polish, Czechoslovakian, and so on. There are a number who achieved most of their victories flying with other formations, such as Americans who later transferred to the USAAF, or some European pilots who had earlier flown with their own air forces. In every case their victory score is that which they achieved in total, not just while with RAF units.

As with the other two books mentioned above, not all the pictures are good, clear portraits. I have in some cases had to rely on poor reproductions, proceeding on the basis that a poor picture is better than no picture at all.

ACKNOWLEDGMENTS

I am honoured to be among friends and colleagues when it comes to sharing information and photographs. While my own collec tion of pictures of the aces is pretty good, having been a collector for some forty years, I knew I would have gaps. I knew too these friends would dig into their own archives and help me try for as complete a collection of faces as could be gathered together. I am pleased to acknowledge their help here. Christopher Shores, Brian Cull, Andrew Thomas, Bjorn Olsen, Wojtek Matusiak, Michael Schoeman, Dave Ross, Chris Thomas, Peter Caygill and Don Minterne. I have also been helped by some pilot's family members, among them are Jacqueline Wilton, David Orton, Richard Doleman, Jennifer Dexter, Pamela Bisdee and Stan Kogel. Thank you one and all.

Norman Franks
East Sussex, England

Abbreviations

AFC	Air Force Cross
AM	Air Medal (U.S.)
BofB	Battle of Britain
CAF	Czechoslovakian Air Force
CdG	Croix de Guerre (Fr)French, (Bel)Belgian)
DFC	Distinguished Flying Cross
DFC(U.S.)	American DFC
DFM	Distinguished Flying Medal
DoI	Died of Injuries
DoW	Died of Wounds
DSC	Distinguished Service Cross (FAA)
DSC	Distinguished Service Cross (U.S.)
DSO	Distinguished Service Order
FAA	Fleet Air Arm
FFAF	Free French Air Force
KIA	Killed in Action
KIFA	Killed in Flying Accident
Ld'H	Legion d'Honneur (French)
Nav/Rad	Navigator/Radar Operator
PAF	Polish Air Force
RAAF	Royal Australian Air Force
RCAF	Royal Canadian Air Force
RNAF	Royal Norwegian Air Force
RNZAF	Royal New Zealand Air Force
SAAF	South African Air Force
USAAF	United States Army Air Force
*	Bar to decoration
**	Two Bars to decoration
***	Three Bars to decoration
++	Clusters to U.S. decoration or (number) the number of clusters (bars) to American DFC or AM

THE PICTORIAL RECORD

Pat
Squadron Leader Marmaduke Thomas StJohn Pattle
DFC*
Born Cape Province, S Africa, 3 July 1914. KIA, Greece, 20 April 1941
80 and 33 Squadrons
Theatres: North Africa; Greece
Approx. 50 and 2 shared victories

Johnnie
Group Captain James Edgar Johnson
DSO** DFC* DFC (US), Order of Leopold (Bel), CdG (Bel)
Born Melton Mowbray, Leicestershire, 9 March 1915. Died 30 January 2001
19, 616 and 610 Squadrons, Kenley, 127 and 144 Wings
Theatres: BofB, Northern France, France & Germany
34 and 7 shared victories

Sailor
Group Captain Adolf Gysbert Malan
DSO* DFC*, Ld'H(Fr), CdG(Fr & Bel), Czech MC
Born Wellington, S Africa, 3 October 1910. Died SA, 17 September 1963
74 Squadron, Biggin Hill Wing
Theatres: Dunkirk, BofB, Northern France
27 and 7 shared victories

Bill
Squadron Leader William Vale
DFC* AFC, DFC (Greek)
From Chatham, Kent. Died in road accident 29 November 1981
33 and 80 Squadrons
Theatres: North Africa, Greece
30 and 3 shared victories

Screwball
Flight Lieutenant George Frederick Beurling
DSO DFC DFM*
Born Montreal, Canada, 6 December 1921. KIFA Rome, 20 May 1948
41, 249 Squadrons, 403 and 412 RCAF Squadrons
Theatres: Northern France, Malta
31 and 1 shared victories

Paddy
Wing Commander Brendan Eamonn Fergus Finucane
DSO DFC**
Born Dublin, Eire, 16 October 1920. KIA Channel, 15 July 1943
65 and 452 RAAF Squadrons, Hornchurch Wing
Theatres: BofB, Northern France
26 and 6 shared victories

Killer
Group Captain Clive Robertson Caldwell
DSO DFC*, Polish Cross of Valor
Born Sydney, Australia, 28 July 1911. Died 5 August 1994
250 and 112 Squadrons, 1 Wing RAAF
Theatres: North Africa, Northern Australia
26 and 4 shared victories

Bob
Wing Commander John Robert Daniel Braham
DSO** DFC* AFC
Born Somerset, England, 6 April 1920. Died Halifax, Canada, 7 February 1974
29, 141, 613, 305, 21 and 107 Squadrons
Theatres: BofB, Night Home Defence, France and Germany
29 victories
(Usual Nav/Rad, F/L William James Gregory DSO DFC AFC DFM: 1913-2001)
('Sticks' Gregory is on the left in the picture.)

Nev
Squadron Leader Neville Frederick Duke
DSO DFC** AFC, Czech War Cross
Born Tunbridge, Kent, 11 January 1922
92, 112, 92 and 145 Squadrons
Northern France, North Africa, Tunisia, Italy
27 and 2 shared victories

Wing Commander Colin Falkland Gray
DSO DFC**
Born Christchurch, NZ, 9 November 1914. Died NZ, 2 August 1995
54, 1, 41 and 81 Squadrons, 322 Wing
Theatres: BofB, Northern France, North Africa, Sicily/Italy
27 and 2 shared victories

Bob
Wing Commander Robert Roland Stanford Tuck
DSO DFC** DFC(US)
Born Catford, London, 1 July 1916. Died Kent, 5 May 1987
92 and 257 Squadrons, Duxford, West Malling and Biggin Hill Wings
Theatres: Dunkirk, BofB, Northern France
27 and 2 shared victories

Chota
Group Captain Frank Reginald Carey
DFC** AFC DFM, Silver Star(US)
Born Brixton, London, 7 May 1912. Died West Sussex, 7 December 2004
43, 3, 43 and 135 Squadrons, 267 and 165 Wings
Theatres: France, BofB, Burma
25 and 3 shared victories

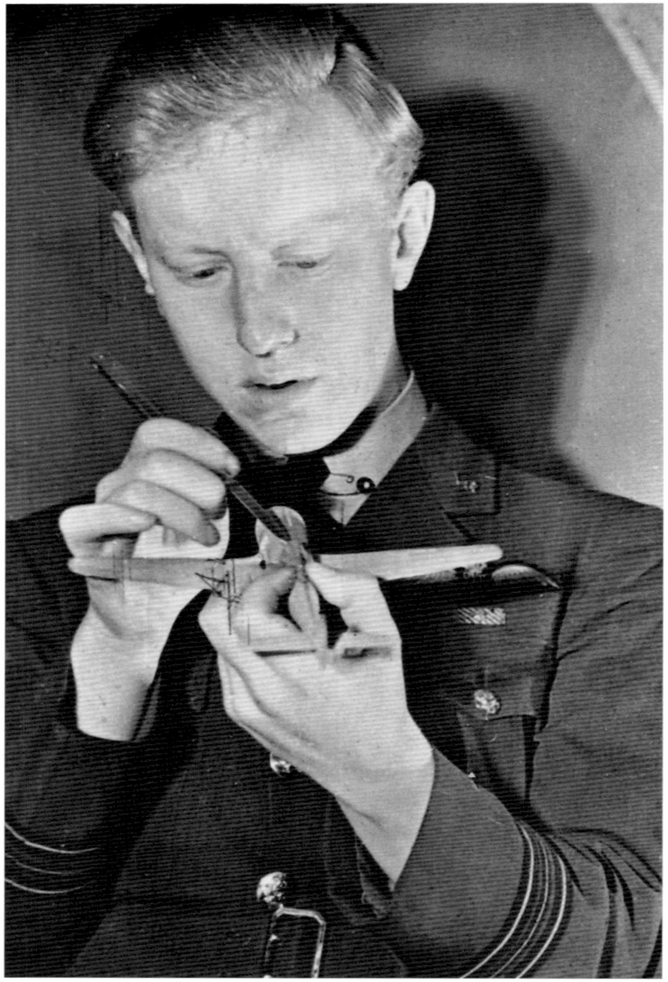

Ginger
Squadron Leader James Henry Lacey
DFM* CdG(Fr)
Born Wetherby, Yorkshire, 1 February 1917. Died 30 May 1989
501, 602 and 17 Squadrons
Theatres: France, BofB, Northern France, Burma
28 victories

Billy
Group Captain Billy Drake
DSO DFC* DFC(US)
Born London, 20 December 1917
1 Squadron, 421 Flight, 128 and 112 Squadrons, Hal Far and 20 Wings
Theatres: France, Northern France, West Africa, North Africa, Malta,
23 and 3 shared victories

Sawn-off Lockie
Flight Lieutenant Eric Stanley Lock
DSO DFC*
Born Shrewsbury, 19 April 1919. KIA, N France, 3 August 1941
41 and 611 Squadrons
Theatres: BofB, Northern France
26 victories

Sheep
Group Captain George Kemp Gilroy
DSO DFC* DFC(US), CdG(Bel)
Born Edinburgh, Scotland, 1 June 1914. Died Scotland, 25 March 1995
603 and 609 Squadrons, 324 Wing
Theatres: BofB, Northern France, Tunisia. Sicily/Italy
14 and 11 shared victories

Wildcat
Wing Commander Lance Cleo Wade
DSO DFC**
Born Broaddus, Texas, USA, 1915. KIFA Foggia, Italy, 12 January 1944
33 and 145 Squadrons
Theatres: North Africa, Tunisia, Italy
23 and 2 shared victories

Tinlegs
Group Captain Douglas Robert Stewart Bader
DSO* DFC*
Born North London, 21 February 1910. Died London, 5 September 1982
19, 222 and 242 Squadrons, Tangmere Wing
Theatres: Dunkirk, BofB, Northern France
20 and 4 shared victories

Raz
Wing Commander Ronald Berry
DSO DFC*
Born Hull, Yorkshire, 3 May 1917. Died September 2000
603 and 81 Squadrons, 322 Wing
Theatres: BofB, North Africa, Tunisia
14 and 10 shared victories
(On the left is W/Cdr J G Sanders DFC (16))

Don
Captain Dominic Salvatore Gentile
DSC* DFC(8), AM(4)
Born Piqua, Ohio, USA, 6 December 1920. KIFA Forestville, Maryland, 28 January 1951
133 Eagle Squadron, 336th Fighter Squadron USAAF
Theatre: Northern Europe
21 and 2 shared victories
(Two victories with RAF)

Don
Wing Commander Donald Ernest Kingaby
DSO DFM** DFC(US) CdG(Bel)
Born Holloway, London, 7 January 1920. Died Westfield, Mass., USA, 31 December 1990
266, 92, 64,122 and 501 Squadrons, Hornchurch Wing
Theatres: BofB, Northern France, Normandy
21 and 2 shared victories

Rosie
Wing Commander Evan Dall Mackie
DSO DFC* DFC(US)
Born Waihi, NZ, 31 October 1917. Died Tauranga, NZ, 28 April 1988
485 NZ Squadron, 243, 92, 274 and 80 Squadrons, 122 Wing
Theatres: Northern France, Tunisia, Sicily/Italy, France & Germany
20 and 3 shared victories

Bill
Wing Commander William Vernon Crawford-Compton
DSO* DFC* Silver Star(US)
Born Invercargill, NZ, 2 March 1916. Died 2 January 1988
485 NZ Squadron, 611, 64 and 122 Squadrons, Hornchurch and 145 Wings
Theatres: Northern France, Normandy
21 and 1 shared victories

Red Knight
Wing Commander Michael Nicholson Crossley
DSO DFC
Born Halford, Warwickshire, 29 May 1912. Died in South Africa, September 1987
32 Squadron
Theatres: France, BofB
20 and 2 shared victories

Tony
Wing Commander Anthony Desmond Joseph Lovell
DSO* DFC* DFC(US)
Born Ceylon, 9 August 1919. KIFA Old Sarum, 17 August 1945
41, 145 Squadrons, 1435 Flt/Sqn, 322 Wing
Theatres: BofB, Northern England, Malta, Italy
16 and 6 shared victories

Des
Wing Commander Desmond Annersley Peter McMullen
DFC**
Born Godstone, Surrey, 6 December 1917. Died 1 July 1985
54, 222, 151, 266, 124 and 65 Squadrons
Theatres: Dunkirk, BofB, Night Home Defence, Northern France
17 and 5 shared victories
(Sitting in front of McMullen is F/Lt J A Leathart DFC(8))

Jamie
Air Commodore James Rankin
DSO* DFC* CdG(Bel)
Born Portabello, Edinburgh, 7 May 1913. Died Edinburgh, 20 March 1975
64 and 92 Squadrons, Biggin Hill Wing
Theatres: Northern France
17 and 5 shared victories

Woody
Wing Commander Vernon Crompton Woodward
DFC*
Born Victoria, BC, Canada, 22 December 1916.
33 Squadron
Theatres: North Africa, Greece
18 and 4 shared victories

Sammy
Flight Lieutenant Geoffrey Allard
DFC DFM*
Born York, 20 August 1912. KIFA Kirton-in-Lindsay, 13 March 1941
85 Squadron
Theatres: France, BofB
16 and 5 shared victories

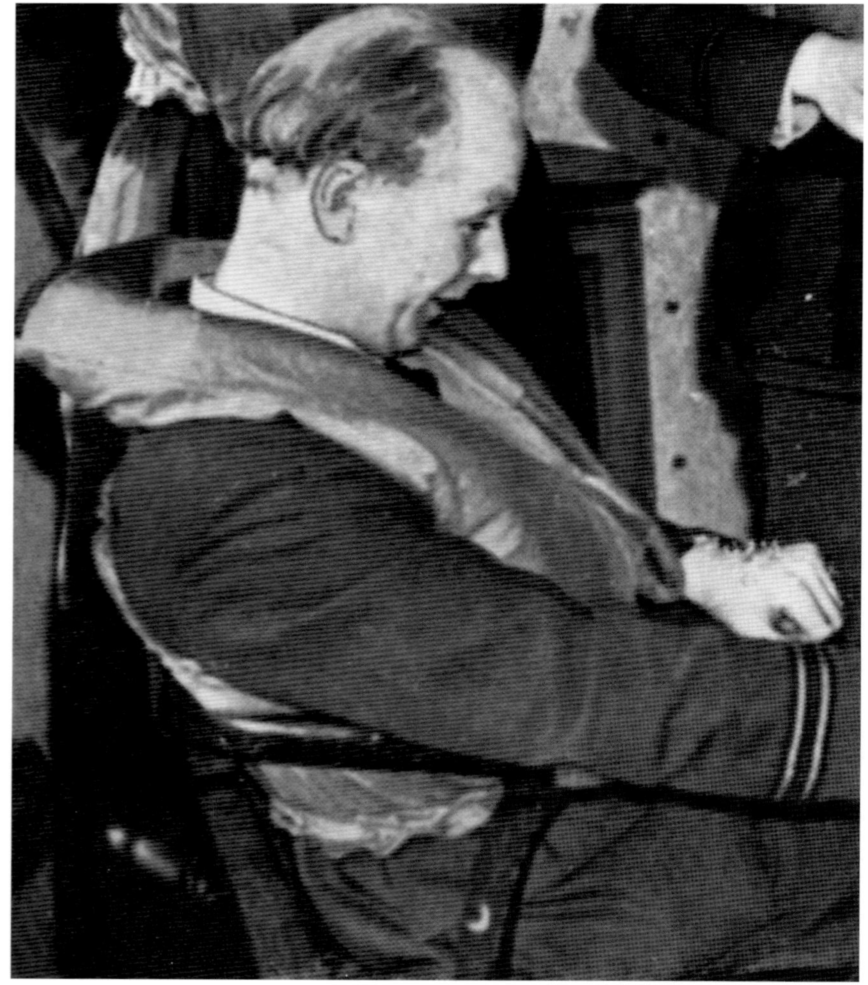

Fin
Group Captain Robert Findlay Boyd
DSO DFC* AE
Born East Kilbride, Scotland, 24 January 1917. Died Skye, April 1975
602 and 54 Squadrons, Kenley Wing, RAF Eglinton, 293 Wing
Theatres: BofB, Northern France, Burma
14 and 7 shared victories

Wing Commander Branse Arthur Burbridge
DSO* DFC* DFC(US)
Born East Dulwich, London, 4 February 1921
85 Squadron
Theatres: Night Home Defence, Night Offence Germany
21 victories
(On the left is his Nav/Rad, S/L Frank Seymour 'Bill' Skelton DSO* DFC*)

Wally
Squadron Leader Henry Wallace McLeod
DSO DFC*
Born in Regina, Canada, 17 December 1915. KIA Holland, 27 September 1944
485 RNZAF Sqn, 411 RCAF Sqn, 603 and 1435 Sqns, 443 RCAF Sqn
Theatres: Northern France, Malta, France and Germany
21 victories

Stan
Wing Commander Stanislaw Skalski
DSO DFC** Virtuti Militari (Gold & Silver), Cross of Valour***
Born Kodyma, Poland, 27 November 1915. Died Warsaw, 12 November 2004
142 Eskadra, 501, 306 and 316 Squadrons, Polish Fighting Team, 133 Wing
Theatres: Poland, BofB, Northern France, Tunisia, Normandy
18 and 3 shared victories

Mike
Wing Commander Maurice Michael Stephens
DSO DFC**
Born Ranchi, India, 20 October 1919. Died 23 September 2004
3, 232, 80, 249 and 229 Squadrons, Hal Far Wing
Theatres: France, BofB, Turkey, North Africa, Malta
18 and 3 shared victories

Cat's Eyes
Group Captain John Cunningham
DSO** DFC*, Silver Star(US), Order of Patriotic War (USSR)
Born Croydon, Surrey, 27 July 1917. Died July 2002
604 and 85 Squadrons
Theatre: Night Home Defence
20 victories
(Nav/Rad, S/Ldr Cecil Frederick 'Jimmy' Rawnsley DSO DFC DFM*)

Gerry
Group Captain Gerald Richmond Edge
OBE DFC
Born 24 September 1913. Died August 2000
605 and 253 Squadrons
Theatres: France, BofB
18 and 2 shared victories
(Edge is on the right)

Dutch
Group Captain Petrus Hendrik Hugo
DSO DFC**, DFC(US), CdG(Fr)
Born Pampoenpoort, Cape Province, SA, 20 December 1917. Died SA, 1986
615 and 41 Squadrons, Tangmere and 322 Wing
Theatres: BofB, Northern France, Tunisia, Sicily/Italy
17 and 3 shared victories

Old Kut
Flight Lieutenant Karel Miroslav Kuttelwascher
DFC* Czech War Cross
Born Svaty Kriz, Czechoslovakia, 23 September 1916. Died Cornwall, England, 17 August 1959
GCIII/6, 1 Squadron
Theatres: France, Northern France
18 and 2 shared victories

Archie
Squadron Leader Archibald Ashmore McKeller
DSO DFC*
Born Paisley, Scotland, 10 April 1912. KIA Kent, 1 November 1940
602 and 605 Squadrons
Theatre: BofB
17 and 3 shared victories

Hilly
Wing Commander Mark Henry Brown
DFC* CdG(Fr) Czech War Cross
Born Glanboro, Manitoba, Canada, 9 October 1911. KIA Sicily, 12 November 1942
1 Squadron, Takali Wing
Theatres: France, BofB, Malta
15 and 4 shared victories

Manfred
Squadron Leader Count Manfred Beckett Czernin
DSO MC DFC
Born Berlin, 18 January 1913. Died London, 6 October 1962
85, 17, 65, 222, 41 and 146 Squadrons (later SOE Italy)
Theatres: France, BofB, Assam
13 and 6 shared victories

Al
Wing Commander Alan Christopher Deere
DSO OBE DFC* DFC(US) CdG(Fr)
Born Auckland, NZ, 12 December 1917. Died England, 20 September 1995
54, 602 and 611 Squadrons, Biggin Hill and 145 Wings
Theatres: Dunkirk, BofB, Northern Europe, Normandy
18 and 1 shared victories

Smithy
Group Captain Wilfred George Gerald Duncan Smith
DSO* DFC**
Born Madras, India, 28 May 1916. Died Devon, 11 December 1996
611, 603, 64 Squadrons, Luqa, 244 and 324 Wings
Theatres: Northern Europe, Sicily/Italy
17 and 2 shared victories

Wing Commander Roy Gilbert Dutton
DSO DFC*
Born Hatton, Ceylon, 2 March 1917. Died 14 September 1988
111, 145, 485 and 19 Squadrons
Theatres: BofB, Northern Europe
13 and 6 shared victories

Jim
Wing Commander Herbert James Lempriere Hallowes
DFC DFM*
Born Lambeth, London, 17 April 1912. Died 20 October 1987
43, 122, 222, 165 and 504 Squadrons
Theatres: BofB, Northern Europe
17 and 2 shared victories

Hess
Flight Lieutenant Raymond Brown Hesselyn
MBE DFC DFM*
Born Dunedin, NZ, 13 March 1921. Died Uxbridge, 14 November 1963
249, 277 and 222 Squadrons
Theatres: Malta, Northern Europe
18 and 1 shared victories

Des
Wing Commander Frederick Desmond Hughes
DSO DFC**
Born Belfast, 6 June 1919. Died Lincolnshire, 11 January 1992
264, 125, 600 and 604 Squadrons
BofB, Night Home Defence, North Africa, France & Germany
18 and 1 shared victories
(Nav/Rad 600 Sqn, P/O L Dixon DFC*)

Willie
Flying Officer William Lidstone McKnight
DFC*
Born Edmonton, Canada, 18 November 1918. KIA France, 12 January 1941
615 and 242 Squadrons
Theatres: France, BofB, Northern Europe
17 and 2 shared victories

Ginger
Group Captain Adrian Hope Boyd
DSO DFC*
Born Sialkot, India, 1 January 1913. Died 21 January 1975
145 and 501 Squadrons, Middle Wallop Wing
Theatres: BofB, Northern Europe, Middle East
15 and 3 shared victories

Moses
Wing Commander Jean-Francois Demozay
DSO DFC* Légion d'Honneur, Ordre de Liberation(Fr), CdG(Fr), DFC(US), CdG(Bel),
Czech War Cross
1, 242 and 91 Squadrons
Theatres: Northern Europe
18 victories

Eddie or Stocky
Wing Commander James Francis Edwards
DFC* DFM
Born Nokomis, Saskatchewan, Canada, 5 June 1921
94, 260 and 92 Squadrons, 127 Wing
Theatres: North Africa, Tunisia, Italy, Normandy, Germany
15 and 3 shared victories

Ray
Wing Commander Raymond Hiley Harries
DSO* DFC** CdG(Fr) CdG(Bel)
Born South Wales, 1916. KIFA Liverpool Bay, 14 May 1950
131 and 91 Squadrons, Tangmere, Westhampnett and 135 Wings
Theatres: Northern Europe, Germany
13 and 5 shared victories

Squadron Leader George Urquhart Hill
DFC**
Born Antigonish, Nova Scotia, 29 October 1918. Killed road accident 12 November 1969
403 RCAF Squadron, 111 Squadron, 441 RCAF Squadron
Theatres: Northern Europe, Tunisia, Sicily
10 and 8 shared victories

Chris
Squadron Leader Johannes Jacobus LeRoux
DFC**
Born Heidelberg, South Africa, 1920. KIFA Channel, 29 August 1944
85, 91, 111 and 602 Squadrons
Theatres: France, Northern Europe, Tunisia, Normandy
18 victories

Flight Lieutenant Alfred Ernest Marshall
DFC DFM
From Hitchin, Hertfordshire, born Portsmouth, 1915. KIFA 27 November 1944
73, 250 and 25 Squadrons
Theatres: France, BofB, North Africa, Night Home Defence
16 and 2 shared victories

Mickey
Wing Commander Michael Lister Robinson
DSO DFC*
Born Chelsea, London, 8 May 1917. KIA Channel, 10 April 1942
87, 601, 238 and 609 Squadrons, Biggin Hill and Tangmere Wings
Theatres: BofB, Northern Europe
18 victories

Bill
Flight Lieutenant William Thomas Edward Rolls
DFC DFM
Born Edmonton, London, 6 August 1914. Died July 1988
72, 122 and 126 Squadrons
Theatres: BofB, Northern Europe, Malta
17 and 1 shared victories

Wing Commander Witold Urbanowicz
DFC, Virtuti Militari (Silver), Cross of Valour***, DFC(US), Air Medal(US)
Chinese Air Cross
Born Olszanka, Poland, 30 March 1908. Died New York, USA, 17 August 1996
111 Eskadra, 145 and 303 Squadrons, 75th US Fighter Squadron
Theatres: Poland, BofB, China
18 victories

Lofty
Flight Lieutenant Brian John George Carbury
DFC*
Born Wellington, NZ, 27 February 1918. Died High Wycombe, UK, 31 July 1961
603 Squadron
Theatre: BofB
15 and 2 shared victories

Tom
Group Captain Thomas Frederick Dalton-Morgan
OBE DSO DFC* Bronze Star(US)
Born Cardiff, 23 March 1917. Died Australia, 18 September 2004
43 Squadron, Middle Wallop and Ibsley Wings
Theatres: BofB, Northern Europe
14 and 3 shared victories

Dan
Squadron Leader Stephen Walter Daniel
DSO DFC*
Born Farnham Common, Slough, 3 April 1920. Died March 1982
72, 601 and 145 Squadrons
Theatres: Northern Europe, North Africa, Sicily/Italy
16 and 1 shared victories
(Daniel is on the right, Neville Duke (28) on the left.)

Dennis
Group Captain William Dennis David
DFC* AFC
Born Surbiton, Surrey, 25 July 1918. Died London, 25 August 2000
87 and 213 Squadrons
Theatres: France, BofB, Ceylon
15 and 2 shared victories

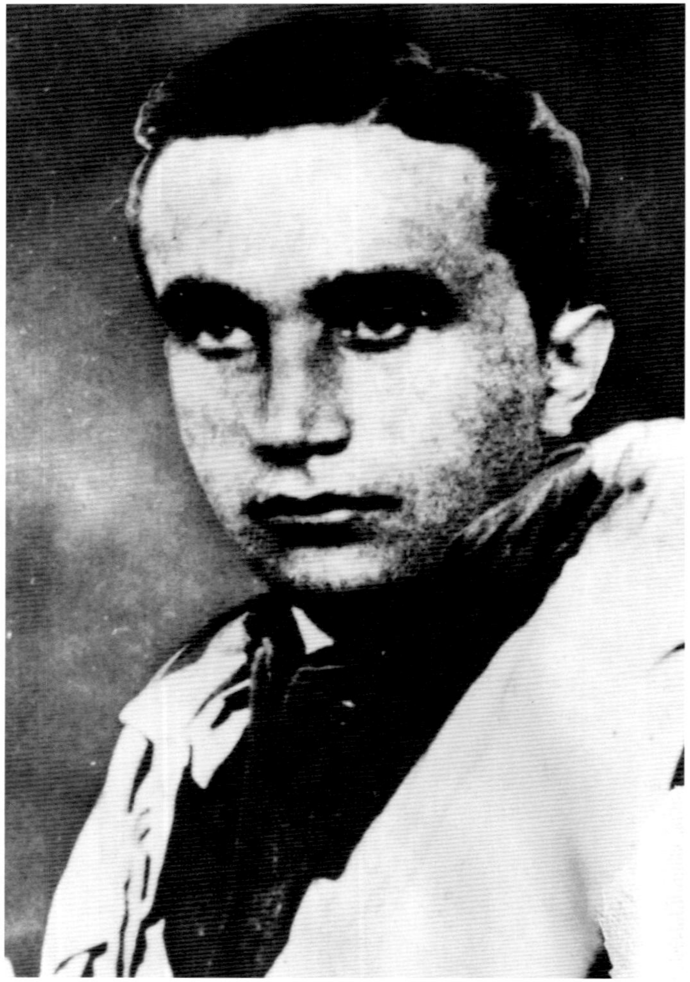

Sergeant Josef Frantisek
DFM* Polish Virtuti Militari and Cross of Valour*** Czech MC
Born Otaslavice, Czechoslovakia, 7 October 1913. KIFA Northolt, 8 October 1940
303 Polish Squadron
Theatre: BofB
17 victories

Mike
Major Boleslaw Michel Gladych
DFC, Silver Star++(US), Air Medal++(US), Virtuti Militari,
Born Warsaw, Poland, 17 May 1910.
303 and 302 Polish Squadrons, 61st Fighter Squadron, USAAF
Theatres: Poland, France, Northern Europe
17 victories
(8 victories with RAF)

Tim
Squadron Leader Adrian Philip Goldsmith
DFC DFM
Born Waverley, NSW, Australia, 25 April 1921. Died 25 March 1961
242, 126 and 452 RAAF Squadrons
Theatres: Northern Europe, Malta, North Australia
16 and 1 shared victories

Little Beak
Squadron Leader Eugeniusz Horbaczewski
DSO DFC* Virtuti Militari (Gold and Silver), Cross of Valour***
Born Kiev, Russia, 28 September 1917. KIA France, 18 August 1944
303 Polish, 145, 43 and 315 Polish Squadrons
Theatres: Northern Europe, Tunisia, Sicily/Italy, Normandy
16 and 1 shared victories

Pat
Flight Lieutenant Paterson Clarence Hughes
DFC
Born Cooma, NSW, Australia, 19 September 1917. KIA 7 September 1940
234 Squadron
Theatre: BofB
14 and 3 shared victories

Johnny
Squadron Leader John Joseph Lynch
DFC*
Born Alhambra, California, USA. KIFA Okinawa, 9 March 1956
71 and 249 Squadrons
Theatres: Northern Europe, Malta
10 and 7 shared victories

Mac/Jay
Squadron Leader James Archibald Findlay MacLachlan
DSO DFC** Czech War Cross
Born Styal, Cheshire, 1 April 1919. DoW France, 31 July 1943
88, 73, 145, 261, 1 Squadrons, AFDU
Theatres: France, Malta, Northern Europe
16 and 1 shared victories

Imshi
Squadron Leader Ernest Michelson Mason
DFC
Born Darlington, County Durham, 29 July 1913. KIA Martuba, N Africa, 15 February 1942
80, 274, 261 and 94 Squadrons
Theatres: North Africa, Iran, Western Desert
15 and 2 shared victories

Don
Flight Lieutenant Donald Alistair Stewart McKay
DFM*
Born Pontefract, Yorkshire, 1917. Died 30 September 1959
501 Squadron, 421 Flight, 91 and 234 Squadrons
Theatres: France, BofB, Northern Europe, North Africa
16 and 1 shared victories

Fanny
Squadron Leader Newell Orton
DFC*
From Warwick, born, 25 August 1915. KIA France, 17 September 1941
73, 242 and 54 Squadrons
Theatres: France, Northern Europe
17 victories

Johnny
Wing Commander John Agorastos Plagis
DSO DFC*
Born Hartley, S Rhodesia, 10 March 1919. Died Rhodesia.
249, 185, 64 and 126 Squadrons
Theatres: Malta, France and Germany
15 and 2 shared victories

Ragbags
Wing Commander Alexander Coultate Rabagliati
DFC*
From Scotland, born 1914. KIA North Sea, 6 July 1943
46, 126 Squadrons, Takali and Coltishall Wings
Theatres: BofB, Malta, North Sea
16 and 1 shared victories

Squadron Leader John Evelyn Scoular
DFC AFC
From Cumbria, born 1911. Died August 1986
73 Squadron, 'K' Flight, 250 Squadron
Theatres: France, North Africa
14 and 3 shared victories

Steve
Wing Commander Harbourne Mackay Stephen
DSO DFC*
Born Elgin, Scotland, 18 April 1916. Died August 2001
74 and 234 Squadrons, 166 Wing
Theatres: Dunkirk, BofB, Northern Europe, Burma
9 and 8 shared victories

Pancho
Squadron Leader John Wolferstan Villa
DFC*
From South Kensington, London. Died 1983
72, 92 and 65 Squadrons
Theatres: BofB, Northern Europe
13 and 4 shared victories

Pete
Group Captain Peter Guy Wykeham-Barnes
DSO* DFC* Danish Order of Dannebrog
Born Sandhurst, Surrey, 13 September 1915. Died March 1995
80, 274, 73, 257 and 23 Squadrons, 140 Wing
Theatres: North Africa, Northern Europe, Sicily, France & Germany
14 and 3 shared victories

Johnny
Group Captain John Robert Baldwin
DSO* DFC*
Born Bath, Somerset, 16 July 1918. KIA, Korea, 15 March 1952
609 and 198 Squadrons, 146 and 123 Wings
Theatres: Northern Europe, Normandy, France & Germany
15 and 1 shared victories

Pete
Wing Commander Peter Malam Brothers
DSO DFC*
Born Prestwich, Lancashire, 30 September 1917.
32, 257, 457 and 602 Squadrons, Tangmere, Exeter and Culmhead Wings
Theatres: BofB, Northern Europe, Normandy
16 victories

Jack
Wing Commander Edward Francis John Charles
DSO DFC* Silver Star(US)
Born Coventry, England, 6 February 1919. Died Vancouver, 5 November 1986
54, 64 and 611 Squadrons, Middle Wallop and Perranporth Wings
Theatres: BofB, Northern Europe
15 and 1 shared victories

Ape
Flight Lieutenant Richard Nigel Cullen
DFC
Born Newcastle, NSW, Australia, 5 June 1917. KIA Himara, Greece, 4 March 1941
80 Squadron
Theatres: North Africa, Greece
15 and 1 shared victories

Capitaine Roland De La Poype
Hero of the Soviet Union, Order of Lenin
Born Pradeaux, France, 28 July 1920
602 Squadron, Normandie-Niéman Regt
Theaters: Northern Europe, Russia
7 and 9 shared victories
(one victory with RAF)

Bob
Squadron Leader Robert Francis Thomas Doe
DFC* Indian DSO
Born Reigate, Surrey, 10 March 1920
234, 238, 66 and 10 RIAF Squadrons
Theatres: BofB, Northern Europe, Burma
14 and 2 shared victories

John
Flight Lieutenant John Charles Dundas
DFC*
Born West Yorkshire, c.1916. KIA off Isle of Wight, 28 November 1940
609 Squadron
Theatres: Dunkirk, BofB
12 and 4 shared victories

Bill
Pilot Officer William Henry Franklin
DFM*
From Poplar, East London, born 2 October 1911. KIA Channel, 12 December 1940
65 Squadron
Theatres: Dunkirk, BofB
13 and 3 shared victories

Jack
Major John Everitt Frost
DFC*
Born Queenstown, Cape Province, S Africa, 16 July 1918. KIA El Adem, Libya, 16 June 1942
3 and 5 SAAF Squadrons
Theatre: East Africa, North Africa
14 and 2 shared victories

Widge
Wing Commander Ian Richard Gleed
DSO DFC CdG(Bel), CdG(Fr)
Born Finchley, London, 3 July 1916. KIA Tunisia, 16 April 1943
266, 87 Squadrons, Ibsley and 244 Wings
Theatres: France, BofB, Northern Europe, Tunisia
13 and 3 shared victories

Benny
Flying Officer George Ernest Goodman
DFC
Born Haifa, Palestine, 8 October 1920. KIA Gazala, 14 June 1941
1 and 73 Squadrons
Theatres: France, BofB, North Africa
10 and 6 shared victories

Captain Svein Heglund
DSO DFC
Born Norway, 10 December 1918. Died Oslo, 18 June 1998
331 Norwegian and 85 Squadrons
Theatres: Northern Europe, France and Germany
15 and 1 shared victories

Ted
Flight Lieutenant Edward William Foott Hewett
AFC DFM
80 Squadron
Theatre: Greece
16 victories

Cobber
Flight Lieutenant Edgar James Kain
DFC
Born Hastings, NZ, 27 June 1918. KIFA Echemines, France, 6 June 1940
73 Squadron
Theatre: France
16 victories

Don
Squadron Leader Donald Currie Laubman
DFC
Born Provost, Alberta, Canada, 16 October 1921
412 RCAF Squadron
Theatre: Northern Europe, France and Germany
14 and 2 shared victories

Gerry
Squadron Leader Albert Gerald Lewis
DFC*
Born Kimberley, South Africa, 10 April 1918. Deceased
85, 249 and 261 Squadrons
Theatres: France, BofB, Ceylon
16 victories

Mac
Squadron Leader John Frederick McElroy
DFC*
Born Port Arthur, Ontario, Canada, 1920
249, 421 and 416 RCAF Squadrons
Theatres: Malta, Normandy
13 and 3 shared victories

Buck
Wing Commander Robert Wendell McNair
DSO DFC** Ld'H(Fr) CdG(Fr)
Born Springfield, Nova Scotia, Canada, 15 May 1919. Died London (UK) 15 January 1971
411 RCAF Squadron, 249 Squadron, 411 and 421 RCAF Squadrons, 126 Wing
Theatres: Northern Europe, Malta, Northern Europe
16 victories

Ginger
Wing Commander Thomas Francis Neil
DFC* Bronze Star(US)
Born Bootle, Lancashire, 14 July 1920
249, 41 Squadron, att'd US 9th Air Force
Theatres: BofB, Malta, Normandy
12 and 4 shared victories

Sandy
Wing Commander James Gilbert Sanders
DFC
Born Richmond, Surrey, 19 June 1914. Died Wimbledon, August 2002
615, 255 Squadrons
Theatres: France, BofB, Night Home Defence
15 and 1 shared victories

Wing Commander John Lloyd Waddy
DFC Air Medal(US)
Born Sydney, Australia, 10 December 1914. Died 17 September 1987
250 and 260 Squadrons, 4 SAAF Squadron, 92 Squadron
Theatre: North Africa
15 and 1 shared victories

Max
Group Captain The Honourable John William Maxwell Aitken
DSO DFC Czech War Cross
Born Montreal, Canada, 5 February 1910. Died 1 May 1985
601 Squadron, att'd 610, 68 and 46 Squadrons, Banff Wing
Theatres: France, Northern Europe, Night Home Defence, Aegean, Norwegian Coast
14 and 1 shared victories

Don
Colonel Donald James Mathew Blakeslee
DSC* SS DFC(7) AM(6) DFC(Br)
Born Fairport Harbour, Ohio, 11 September 1917
401 RCAF and 133 Eagle Squadrons, 335th US Fighter Squadron, 4th Fighter Group
Theatre: Northern Europe
14 and 1 shared victories
(6 with RAF)

Bunny
Wing Commander Christopher Frederick Currant
DSO DFC* CdG(Bel)
Born Luton, Bedfordshire, 14 December 1911. Died 12 March 2006
605 and 501 Squadrons, 122 Wing
Theatres: BofB, Northern Europe, Normandy
10 and 5 shared victories

Wing Commander John Ellis
DFC*
Born Deal, Kent, 28 February 1917
610 Squadron, Krendi Wing
Theatres: BofB, Malta
13 and 2 shared victories

Prosser
Group Captain Peter Prosser Hanks
DSO DFC
From York, born 29 July 1917. Died Natal, S Africa, 31 January 1986
1, 257 and 56 Squadrons, Coltishall, Luqa and 286 Wings
Theatres: France, BofB, Northern Europe, Malta, Italy
11 and 4 shared victories

Hap
Squadron Leader Irving Farmer Kennedy
DFC*
Born Cumberland, Ontario, Canada, 4 February 1920
249, 185, 111, 93 and 401 RCAF Squadrons
Theatres: Malta, Sicily/Italy, Normandy
10 and 5 shared victories

Bill
Squadron Leader William Thomas Klersy
DSO DFC*
Born Brantford, Ontario, Canada, 30 July 1922. KIFA 22 May 1945
401 RCAF Squadron
Theatres: Northern Europe, Normandy, France & Germany
14 and 1 shared victories

Dickie
Wing Commander Richard Maxwell Milne
DFC*
Born Edinburgh, Scotland, 8 July 1919
151 and 92 Squadrons, Biggin Hill Wing
Theatres: France, BofB, Northern Europe
14 and 1 shared victories

Ginger
Squadron Leader Alan Joseph Owen
DFC* DFM
Born Chelsea, London, 8 July 1922. Died October 1995
Theatres: North Africa, Tunisia, Night Home Defence, Germany
15 victories
(Nav/Rad F/O James Samuel Victor 'Mac' McAllister DFC* DFM 1918-1995)
(McAllister is on the left)

Bobby
Wing Commander Robert Wardlow Oxspring
DFC**
Born Sheffield, Yorkshire, 22 May 1919. Died 8 August 1989
66, 41, 91 and 72 Squadrons, 24, 141 and Detling Wings
Theatres: BofB, Northern Europe, Tunisia, France & Germany
13 and 2 shared victories

Geoff
Wing Commander Alan Geoffrey Page
DSO DFC*
Born Boxmoor, Hertforshire, 16 May 1920. Died 3 August 2000
56 Squadron, AFDU, 122 and 132 Squadrons, 125 Wing
Theatres: BofB, Northern Europe, Normandy
10 and 5 shared victories

Marshal Budenny
Squadron Leader Francis Joseph Soper
DFC DFM
From Devonport, Devon, born 29 July 1912. KIA 5 October 1941
1 and 257 Squadrons
11 and 4 shared victories

Flight Lieutenant Gray Stenborg
DFC
Born Auckland, NZ, 13 October 1921. KIA France, 24 September 1943
111, 185 and 91 Squadrons
Theatres: Northern Europe, Malta, Northern Europe
14 and 1 shared victories

Steve
Flight Lieutenant Richard Payne Stevens
DSO DFC*
Born Tonbridge, Kent in 1909. KIA Holland, 16 December 1941
151 and 253 Squadrons
Theatres: Night Home Defence, Northern Europe
14 and 1 shared victories

Johnny
Squadron Leader John Stuart Taylor
DFC*
From Suffolk, born c.1920. KIA Sicily, 12 July 1943
145 and 601 Squadrons
Theatres: North Africa, Tunisia, Sicily
13 and 2 shared victories

Grumpy
Flight Lieutenant George Cecil Unwin
DFM*
Born Bolton-on-Dearne, Yorkshire, 18 January 1913. Died 28 June 2006
19 and 613 Squadrons
Theatres: Dunkirk, BofB, Northern Europe
13 and 2 shared victories

Ian
Wing Commander John Watson Allan
DSO DFC
Born Cathcart, Scotland, 1910. Died July 1988
256, 151 and 29 Squadrons
Theatre: Night Fighter - Sicily, Northern Europe
14 victories
(Nav/Rad was F/Lt Harold James Davidson DFC* RAAF)

Butch
Wing Commander Robert Alexander Barton
OBE DFC*
Born Kamloops, BC, Canada, 7 June 1916.
249 Squadron
Theatres: BofB, Malta
10 and 4 shared victories

Cas
Flight Lieutenant Charles Edward Casbolt
DFM
Born Sunderland in 1914.
80 and 250 Squadrons
Theatres: Greece, North Africa
13 and 1 shared victories

Johnny
Wing Commander John Milne Checketts
DSO DFC Silver Star(US), Cross of Valour(Pol)
Born Invercargill, NZ, 20 February 1912. Died NZ, 21 April 2006
611, 485 RNZAF Squadrons, 142 Wing
Theatres: Northern Europe, Normandy, France & Germany
13 and 1 shared victories
(Checketts stands with Bill Jordan, NZ High Commissioner in London)

Moose
Wing Commander Robert Carl Fumerton
DFC*
Born Fort Coulonge, Quebec, Canada, 21 March 1913. Died 10 July 2006
406 RCAF Squadron, 89 Squadron
Theatre: Night Home Defence, Malta, Northern Europe
14 victories
(Nav/Rad FO Leslie Patrick Sandford Bing DFC* RCAF)
(Fumerton left, Bing right)

Tony
Squadron Leader Frederick Anthony Owen Gaze
DFC**
Born Melbourne, Australia, 3 February 1920
610, 616, 64, 129, 610 and 41 Squadrons
Theatres: Northern Europe, France & Germany
11 and 3 shared victories

Peter
Wing Commander Wilfrith Peter Green
DSO DFC
Born Raniknet, India, 1914. KIFA nr. Amiens, France, 1 March 1945
85, 410 RCAF, 96 and 219 Squadrons
Theatres: Night Home Defence, France & Germany
14 victories
(Nav/Rad 219 Sqn, F/L D Oxby DFC DFM)

Jack
Flight Lieutenant Roy Jack Hubert Hussey
DFC DFM
Born Wells, Somerset, 1922. KIFA Dallachy, Scotland, 20 February 1945
72 and 19 Squadrons
Theatres: North Africa, Tunisia, Sicily/Italy, UK
10 and 4 shared victories

Bruce
Squadron Leader Mervin Robert Bruce Ingram
DFC
Born Dunedin, NZ, 13 December 1921. DOAS Burma, 11 July 1944
611, 601, 243 and 152 Squadrons
Theatres: Northern Europe, Malta, North Africa, Italy, Burma
8 and 6 shared victories

Captaine Albert Littolf
Born Cornimont, Vosges, France, 31 October 1911. KIA Russia, 16 July 1943
GCIII/7, 33, 73 and 274 Squadrons, Normandie-Niémen Regt
Theatres: France, North Africa, Greece/Crete, Russia
6 and 8 shared victories
(5 with RAF)

Reg
Flight Lieutenant Reginald Thomas Llewellyn
DFM
Born Bristol, 25 March 1914
213 Squadron
Theatre: BofB
13 and 1 shared victories

Stan
Lieutenant-Commander Stanley Gordon Orr
DSC**
From West London, born 28 September 1916
806 and 804 FAA Squadrons
Theatres: Mediterranean, Norway
7 and 7 shared victories

Wing Commander Nevil Everard Reeves
DSO DFC*
From Naunton, Warwickshire, born 1920. KIFA Norfolk, 27 January 1949
89 and 239 Squadrons, BSDU
Theatres: Night Defence Malta, North Africa, Northern Europe
14 victories
(Nav/Rad was PO Arthur Alexander O'Leary DFC** DFM)
(Reeves left; right is Doug Oxby DSO DFC DFM* (22) Nav/Rad to M C Shipard (13))

Charlie
Squadron Leader Charles Curnow Scherf
DSO DFC*
Born Emmeville, NSW, Australia, 17 May 1917.
Killed road accident, Emmaville, NSW, 13 July 1949
418 RCAF Squadron
Theatre: Day and Night Intruder – Northern Europe
13 and 1 shared victories

Rod
Squadron Leader Roderick Illingworth Alpine Smith
DFC*
From Regina, Canada, born 1 March 1922. Died Vancouver, 14 April 2002
126 Squadron, 412 and 401 RCAF Squadrons
Theatres: Northern Europe, Malta, France & Germany
13 and 1 shared victories

Jas
Wing Commander James Eric Storrar
DFC*
Born Ormskirk, Lancashire, 24 July 1920. Died Chester, April 1995
145 Squadron, 451 Flight, 73, 65, 64, 165 and 234 Squadrons
Theatres: BofB, North Africa, France & Germany
12 and 2 shared victories

Bluey
Squadron Leader Keith William Truscott
DFC*
Born Praham, Victoria, Australia, 17 May 1916. KIFA 28 March 1943
452 and 76 RAAF Squadrons
Theatres: Northern Europe, New Guinea, Darwin
14 victories

Stan
Group Captain Percival Stanley Turner
DSO DFC*
Born Ivybridge, Devon, 3 September 1913. Died Ottawa, 23 July 1985
242, 145 and 249 Squadrons, 417 RCAF Squadron, 244 Wing
Theatres: France, BofB, Northern Europe, Malta, Sicily/Italy
13 and 1 shared victories

Wing Commander Alois Vasatko
DFC, Czech War Cross**, LdH(Fr), CdG(Fr)
Born Celakovice, Czechoslovakia, 25 August 1908. KIA Channel, 23 June 1942
GCI/G, 312 Czech Squadron, Exeter Wing
Theatres: France, Northern Europe
4 and 10 shared victories

Bob
Squadron Leader Robert James Clarendon Whittle
DFM
Born Brisbane, Australia, 10 July 1914
250 Squadron, 86 RAAF Squadron
Theatres: North Africa, New Guinea
11 and 3 shared victories

Pat
Flying Officer Patrick Philip Woods-Scawen
DFC
Born Karachi, India, 29 June 1916. KIA 1 September 1940
85 Squadron
Theatre: France, BofB
10 and 3 shared victories

Allan
Wing Commander Allan Richard Wright
DFC*
Born Teignmouth, Devon, 12 February 1920
92 and 29 Squadrons
Theatres: BofB, Northern Europe, Night Home Defence
11 and 3 shared victories
(Wright centre, flanked by Tony Bartley (13) and Brian Kingcome (12))

Jan
Squadron Leader Jan Eugeniusz Ludwik Zumbach
DFC*, Virtuti Militari (silver), Cross of Valour***
Born Warsaw, Poland, 14 April 1915. Died France, 3 January 1986
GCII/55, 303 Polish Squadron, 133 Wing
Theatres: France, BofB, Northern Europe
12 and 2 shared victories

Tony
Squadron Leader Anthony Charles Bartley
DFC*
Born Dacca, India, 28 March 1919. Died April 2001
92, 65 and 111 Squadrons
Theatres: Dunkirk, BofB, Northern Europe, Tunisia
12 and 1 shared victories

Mindy
Wing Commander Minden Vaughan Blake
DSO DFC
Born Newman Eketchuna, NZ, 13 February 1913. Died Surrey, 30 November 1981
238 and 234 Squadrons, Portreath Wing
Theatres: BofB, Northern Europe
10 and 3 shared victories

Broady
Air Vice Marshal Harry Broadhurst
DSO* DFC* AFC
Born Frimley, Surrey, 28 October 1905. Died West Sussex, 30 August 1995
111 Squadron, 60 Wing, Hornchurch Wing
Theatres: France, Northern Europe
13 victories
(Broadhurst is on the left, G/C Pat Jameson DSO DFC* (9) on the right)

Buck
Wing Commander John Kenneth Buchanan
DSO DFC*
Born Southsea, Hampshire, 19 March 1918. Lost 16 February 1944
37, 272 and 227 Squadrons
Theatre: Bomber Command (UK), Middle East, Malta, Aegean
10 and 3 shared victories

Ed
Wing Commander Edward Dixon Crew
DSO DFC*
Born Higham Ferrers, Northamptonshire, 24 December 1917. Died August 2002
604, 85 and 96 Squadrons
Theatres: Night Home Defence
12 and 1 shared victories
(Nav/Rad 604 Sqn, Sgt N H Guthrie DFM; 85 Sqn F/L B G Duckett DFC)

Johnny
Flight Lieutenant John Curchin
DFC
Born Hawthorne, Victoria, Australia, 20 January 1918. KIA Channel, 4 June 1941
609 Squadron
Theatres: BofB, Northern Europe
8 and 5 shared victories

Hamish
Flight Lieutenant James Dodds
Born Knightswood, Glasgow, Scotland, 22 July 1921
DFM
274 Squadron
Theatre: North Africa
13 victories

Foob
Squadron Leader David Charles Fairbanks
DFC**
From Ithaca, New York, USA, born 22 August 1922. Deceased
501, 274, 3 and 274 Squadrons
Theatres: Normandy, France & Germany
12 and 1 shared victories

Ronnie
Squadron Leader Ronald Henry Fokes
DFC DFM
From Hillingdon, Middlesex, born c.1913. KIA France, 12 June 1944
92, 154, 56, 193 and 257 Squadrons
Theatres: BofB, Northern Europe, Normandy
9 and 4 shared victories

Johnny
Wing Commander John Connell Freeborn
DFC*
From Middleton, Leeds, born 1 December 1919.
74, 602 and 118 Squadrons, 286 Wing
Theatres: BofB, Northern Europe, Italy
12 and 1 shared victories

Johnny
Squadron Leader John Albert Axel Gibson
DSO DFC
Born Brighton, Sussex, 24 August 1916. Died Nottingham, July 2000
501, 457 RAAF, 15 RNZAF and 80 Squadrons
Theatres: France, BofB, Northern Europe, South Pacific, France & Germany
12 and 1 shared victories

Ronnie
Lieutenant-Colonel Ronald Cuthbert Hay
DSO DSC*
Born Perth, Scotland, 4 October 1916. Died Wiltshire, December 2001
801 and 808 FAA Squadrons, 47 Naval Wing
Theatres: Norwegian Coast, Mediterranean, Ceylon, South Pacific Fleet
4 and 9 shared victories

Bert
Squadron Leader Albert Ulric Houle
DFC*
Born Massey, Ontario, Canada, 24 March 1914
213, 145 and 417 RCAF Squadrons
Theatres: North Africa, Italy
12 and 1 shared victories

Johnny
Flight Lieutenant John MacKay
DFC*
Born Winnipeg, Canada (family name Mahachak), 1920
401 RCAF Squadron
Theatre: France & Germany
11 and 2 shared victories

Ken
Flight Lieutenant Kenneth William Mackenzie
DFC
Born Belfast, Northern Ireland, 8 June 1916
501 and 247 Squadrons
Theatres: BofB, Northern Europe
10 and 3 shared victories

Bill
Flight Lieutenant William Ivan Hartley Maguire
DFC*
From Southern Rhodesia, born Bulawayo, 1921
253, 81 and 154 Squadrons
Theatres: Night Home Defence, Tunisia, Sicily/Italy, Cyprus
13 victories

Andy
Wing Commander Andrew McDowell
DFM*
Born Kirkinner, Wigtownshire, Scotland in 1913. Died 26 November 1981
602, 245, 232 and 616 Squadrons
Theatres: BofB, Germany
11 and 2 shared victories

Flight Lieutenant Edward Brian Mortimer-Rose
DFC*
From Littleport, Cambridgeshire, born c.1920. KIFA Tunisia, 28 January 1943
234, 249, 185 and 111 Squadrons
Theatres: BofB, Malta, Tunisia
9 and 4 shared victories

Johnny
Squadron Leader John Colin Mungo-Park
DFC*
Born Wallasey, Cheshire, 1918. KIA France, 27 June 1941
74 Squadron
Theatres: BofB, Northern Europe
11 and 2 shared victories

Orange
Squadron Leader James Joseph O'Meara
DSO DFC*
Born Barnsley, Yorkshire, 20 February 1919
64, 72 Squadrons, 421 Flight, 91, 64 and 131 Squadrons
Theatres: BofB, Northern Europe
11 and 2 shared victories

Wing Commander Marian Pisarek
DFC, Virtuti Militari (Gold and Silver), Cross of Valour***
Born Losie, Poland, 3 January 1912. KIA France, 29 April 1942
141 Eskadra, 303, 308 PAF Squadrons, 1 Polish Wing
Theatres: Poland, BofB, Northern Europe
11 and 2 shared victories

Jack
Flight Lieutenant John Donald Rae
DFC*
Born Auckland, NZ, 15 January 1919
485 RNZAF Squadron, 603 and 249 Squadrons
Theatres: Northern Europe, Malta
11 and 2 shared victories

Smokey
Wing Commander Warren Edward Schrader
DFC*
Born Wellington, NZ, 27 March 1921
1435, 486 RNZAF and 616 Squadrons
Theatres: Malta, France & Germany
11 and 2 shared victories

Jackie
Lieutenant-Commander Alfred Jack Sewell
DSC
KIFA Maine, USA, 3 October 1943
806, 804 and 1837 FAA Squadrons
Theatre: Mediterranean
6 and 7 shared victories

Squadron Leader John Bean Shepherd
DFC**
From Edinburgh, Scotland, born c.1920. KIFA Germany, 22 January 1946
234, 118, 610 and 41 Squadrons
Theatres: Northern Europe, France and Germany
8 and 5 shared victories

Merv
Flight Lieutenant Mervyn Charles Shipard
DFC*
Born Albury, NSW, Australia, 24 July 1917
68 and 89 Squadrons
Theatres: Home Night Defence, Night Ops. Malta, Egypt, North Africa
13 victories
(main Nav/Rad F/O D Oxby DFC DFM (see N E Reeves(14))

Wilf
Wing Commander Wilfred Max Sizer
DFC*
Born Chelmsford, Essex, 23 February 1920
213, 152 and 93 Squadrons
Theatres: France, BofB, Tunisia, Sicily
7 and 6 shared victories

Ted
Squadron Leader Edward Rowland Thorn
DFC DFM*
Born Portsmouth, Hampshire, 1913. KIFA Cambridgeshire, 12 February 1946
264, 32, 169 Squadrons
Theatres: Dunkirk, BofB, Night Home Defence
12 and 1 shared victories
(His air gunner was Sgt Frederick James Barker DFM*)
(Thorne on the left, Barker on right)

Johnny
Wing Commander John Groves Topham
DSO DFC*
Born Bradford, Yorkshire, 18 March 1917. Died 27 February 1987
219 and 125 Squadrons
Theatre: Night Home Defence
13 victories
(Nav/Rad F/Lt Horace Walter William Berridge DSO DFC*)

Jack
Flight Lieutenant John Howard Turnbull
DFC*
Born St Thomas, Ontario, Canada, 30 December 1915
125 and 600 Squadrons
Theatres: Night Home Defence, Night Fighter Tunisia, Sicily/Italy
12 and 1 shared victories
(Nav/Rad was PO Cecil Frank James Fowler DFM*)

Pilot Officer Claud Weaver III
DFC DFM*
Born Oklahoma City, USA, 18 August 1923. KIA France, 28 January 1943
185, and 403 RCAF Squadrons
Theatres: Malta, Northern Europe
12 and 1 shared victories

Terry
Flight Lieutenant John Terrance Webster
DFC
From Liverpool, born 1916. KIA 5 September 1940
41 Squadron
Theatre: BofB
11 and 2 shared victories

Jeff
Squadron Leader Jefferson Heyward Wedgwood
DFC*
From London, born 28 May 1917. KOAS 17 December 1942
253, 80 and 92 Squadrons
Theatres: BofB, North Africa
10 and 3 shared victories

Mike
Squadron Leader Michael Hugh Young
DFC
Born Gloucester, 12 June 1920
264, 73 and 213 Squadrons
Theatres: Dunkirk, BofB, North Africa
7 and 6 shared victories

Harry
Pilot Officer Harold Derrick Atkinson
DFC
From Wintringham, Yorkshire, born 19 August 1918. KIA Portland, 25 August 1940
213 Squadron
Theatre: France, BofB
9 and 3 shared victories

Benny
Squadron Leader George Harman Bennions
DFC
Born Burslem, Staffs, 15 March 1913. Died Yorkshire, 30 January 2004
41 Squadron
Theatre: BofB
12 victories

Wilf
Wing Commander Wilfred Greville Clouston
DFC
Born Auckland, NZ, 15 January 1916. Died 24 May 1980
19, 258 and 488 RNZAF Squadrons
Theatres: Dunkirk, BofB, Singapore
9 and 3 shared victories

Stan
Flight Lieutenant Stanley Dudley Pearce Connors
DFC*
Born Calcutta, India, 8 April 1912. KIA 18 August 1940
111 Squadron
Theatre: France, BofB
12 victories

Lanky
Flight Lieutenant Nicholas Gresham Cooke
DFC
From Blakeney, Norfolk, born 26 August 1913. KIA 31 May 1940
264 Squadron
Theatre: Dunkirk
9 and 3 shared victories
(Air Gunner Cpl Albert Lippett DFM – KIA 31 May 1940)
(Cooke behind, Lippett in front)

Tom
Squadron Leader Thomas Paul Michael Cooper-Slipper
DFC
From Kinver, Staffs, born 11 January 1921. Died Vancouver, 23 February 2004
605, 135 and 232 Squadrons, 103 MU
Theatres: BofB, Malaya, Egypt
9 and 3 shared victories

Len
Flying Officer Leonard Cottingham
DFC
Born Market Rasen, Lincs, 7 February 1916. Deceased early 1980s
33 Squadron
Theatres: North Africa, Greece
11 and 1 shared victories

Mike
Flight Lieutenant Michael Metcalfe Davison
DFC*
Born Tonbridge Wells, 30 June 1922. KIFA 29 February 1964
46, 108 and 264 Squadrons
Theatre: Night Defence North Africa, Sicily, Normandy
12 victories
(Nav/Rad was F/O A C Willmott DFC*)
(NO PHOTO AVAILABLE)

Pilot Officer Count Rodolphe Ghislain Charles De Hemricourt De Grunne
CdG(Bel) Cruz Militar (Spain)
Born Brussels, Belgium, 18 November 1911. KIA Channel, 21 May 1941
(Spanish Civil War), 32 and 609 Squadrons
Theatres: BofB, Northern Europe
11 and 1 shared victories
(2 and 1 shared with RAF)

Dolly
Squadron Leader Robert Daniel Doleman
DSO DFC
Born Dublin, Eire, 7 July 1921. Died 19 August 1972
29 and 157 Squadrons
Theatres: Biscay, Night Fighter – Germany
10 and 2 shared victories
(His Nav/Rad was F/Lt Douglas Campbell Bunch DSO DFC* 1920-72)
(Bunch left, Doleman on the right)

Ace
Flight Lieutenant Alwyn Berriman Downing
DFC DFM, Air Medal(US)
Born Wimbledon, 3 October 1922. Died 22 September 1995
141 and 600 Squadrons
Theatres: Night Fighting, North Africa, Italy, Germany
12 victories
(Nav/Rad FL John Thomas Lyons DFC DFM AM c.1913-44)
(Lyons left, and Downing receiving Air Medals from Maj-Gen. E J House, OC 12th US AF Support Command)

Bobby
Wing Commander Robert Henry Maxwell Gibbes
DSO DFC*
Born Balgowlash, NSW, Australia, 6 May 1916
3 RAAF Squadron, 80 Wing
Theatres: North Africa, SW Pacific
10 and 2 shared victories

Tom
Squadron Leader Thomas Grier
DFC
Born Glasgow, 1918. KIA Le Havre, 5 December 1941
601 and 32 Squadrons
Theatres: BofB, Northern Europe
8 and 4 shared victories

Len
Flying Officer Leonard Archibald Haines
DFC
Born Melcombe Regis, Dorset. KIFA 30 April 1941
19 Squadron
Theatres: Dunkirk, BofB
8 and 4 shared victories

Ossie
Squadron Leader Osgood Villiers Hanbury
DSO DFC*
From Herriard, Hampshire, c.1918. KOAS Biscay, 3 June 1943
602 and 260 Squadrons
Theatres: BofB, North Africa, Tunisia
10 and 2 shared victories

Taffy
Flight Lieutenant Frederick William Higginson
DFC DFM
Born Swansea, S Wales, 17 February 1913. Died 12 February 2002
56 Squadron
Theatres: France, BofB, Northern Europe
12 victories

Hodge
Flight Lieutenant Arthur John Hodgkinson
DSO DFC*
From Hampstead, London, born 1916. KIA Rome, 10 July 1943
219, 264 and 23 Squadrons
Theatres: Night Home Defence, BofB, Night Intruder Sicily/Italy
12 victories
(Nav/Rad (219 Sqn) was Sgt Bertram Ernest Dye DFM*)

Sub-Lieutenant Graham Angus Hogg
DSC*
Born Shotley Bridge, Newcastle on Tyne, 3 May 1921. KIFA 19 March 1942
806 FAA Squadron
Theatres: Norway, Dunkirk, Mediterranean, Syria
4 and 8 shared victories

Sergeant Harold Norman Howes
DFM
From Gillingham, Kent, born c.1916. KIFA 22 December 1940
85 and 605 Squadrons
Theatres: France, BofB
11 and 1 shared victories

Robin
Wing Commander George Robert Arthur McGarel Johnston
DSO DFC* AE
Born Bloemfontein, S Africa, 2 September 1916. Died March 1992
73 and 65 Squadrons, 122 Wing
Theatres: North Africa, Northern Europe
10 and 2 shared victories

Keefe
Wing Commander George Clinton Keefer
DSO* DFC* CdG(Fr), Netherlands Flying Cross
Born New York City, USA, 11 July 1921. Died Montreal, January 1985
274, 412 RCAF Squadrons, 126 and 125 Wings
Theatres: North Africa, Northern Europe, France & Germany
12 victories

Johnny
Group Captain John Alexander Kent
DSO DFC* AFC Virtuti Militari(Pol)
Born Winnipeg, Canada, 23 June 1914. Died 7 October 1985
303 PAF Squadron, 92 Squadron, Northolt and Kenley Wings
Theatres: BofB, Northern Europe, Middle East
12 victories

Iggy/Killy
Wing Commander John Ignatius Kilmartin
DFC
Born Dundalk, Eire, 8 July 1913. Died 1 October 1989
1, 43, 128 and 504 Squadrons, Hornchurch and 136 Wings
Theatres: France, BofB, West Africa, Northern Europe
10 and 2 shared victories

Brian
Group Captain Charles Brian Fabris Kingcome
DSO DFC*
Born Calcutta, India, 31 May 1917. Died London, UK, 14 February 1994
92 and 72 Squadrons, Kenley and 244 Wings
Theatres: BofB, Northern Europe, Sicily/Italy
9 and 3 shared victories

Wing Commander Howard Clive Mayers
DSO DFC*
Born Sydney, Australia, 9 January 1910. DOAS 20 July 1942
601 and 94 Squadrons, 239 Wing
Theatres: BofB, North Africa
11 and 1 shared victories
(Mayers is on the right, with FO H T Gilbert DFC (5))

Pete
Pilot Officer Peter Alfred Nash
DFC
From Beckenham, Kent, born c.1922. KIA, Malta, 17 May 1942
65, 609 and 249 Squadrons
Theatres: Northern Europe, Malta
11 and 1 shared victories

Flying Officer Frantisek Perina
Czech War Cross, Ld'H(Fr), CdG(Fr)
Born Mokruvsky, Czechoslovakia, 8 April 1911
GCI/5, 312 Czech Squadron
Theatres: France, BofB, Northern Europe
3 and 9 shared victories
(1 victory with RAF)
(Alois Vasatko (14) left, Perina on the right)

Bill
Wing Commander William Riley
DFC
From Manor Hamilton, Eire, born c.1917. KOAS, Mediterranean, 16 July 1942
263, 302 Polish, 145, 252 and 272 Squadrons
Theatres: Norwegian Coast, BofB, Mediterranean
9 and 3 shared victories

Fred
Flying Officer Frederick Neal Robertson
DFM
Born Lockerley, Wiltshire, c.1918. KIFA nr. Norwich, 31 August 1943
66, 261, 219, 153 and 96 Squadrons
Theatres: Dunkirk, Malta, Night Home Defence
11 and 1 shared victories

Paddy
Flying Officer Patrick Alfred Schade
DFM
Born Singapore, Malaya, c.1921. KOAS Sussex, 31 July 1944
501, 54, 126 and 91 Squadrons
Theatres: Malta, Northern Europe
12 victories

Dimsie
Squadron Leader Donald William Alfred Stones
DFC*
Born Norwich, Norfolk, 19 June 1921. Died Hampshire, 22 October 2002
79, 249, MNFU, 605, 155 and 67 Squadrons
Theatres: France, BofB, Malta, Burma
7 and 5 shared victories

Paddy
Squadron Leader Robert Wilkinson Turkington
DSO DFC*
Irish, born Mhow, India, 1920. KIFA Italy, 29 July 1945
43, 72 and 241 Squadrons
Theatres: Tunisia, Italy
9 and 3 shared victories

Pete
Squadron Leader Peter St George Bruce Turnbull
DFC
Born Armidale, NSW, Australia, 9 February 1917. KIA New Guinea, 27 August 1942
3 RAAF Squadron, 75 and 76 RAAF Squadrons
Theatres: North Africa, Syria, New Guinea
12 victories

Squadron Leader Harold Edward Walmsley
DFC*
Born Preston, Lancashire, 14 December 1922
611, 132, 130 and 350 (Belgian) Squadrons
Theatres: Northern Europe, France and Germany
11 and 1 shared victories

Hawkeye
Wing Commander Edward Preston Wells
DSO DFC*
Born Cambridge, North Island, NZ, 26 July 1916. Died 4 November 2005
41, 485 (NZ) Squadrons, Kenley and Tangmere Wings
Theatres: BofB, Northern Europe
12 victories

Harry
Flight Lieutenant Harold Edward White
DFC**
Born 23 May 1923. Died 25 March 1990
141 Squadron, BSDU
Theatres: Offensive Night Operations Northern Europe and Germany
12 victories
(His Nav/Rad was F/Lt Michael Seamer Allen DFC** 1923-2001)
(White is on the left, Mike Allen on the right)

Timber
Wing Commander Eric Norman Woods
DFC*
Born Buenos Aires, Argentina, 8 May 1910. KIA Yugoslavia, 16 December 1943
124, 72, 249 Squadrons, 286 Wing
Theatres: Northern Europe, Malta, Italy and Balkans
10 and 2 shared victories

Slim
Flight Lieutenant John William Yarra
DFM
Born Stanhope, Queensland, 24 August 1921. KIA, Dutch coast, 10 December 1942
185, 453 RAAF Squadrons
Theatres: Malta, Northern Europe
12 victories

Sinker
Squadron Leader Hugo Throssell Armstrong
DFC*
Born Perth, Western Australia, 9 June 1916. KIA Channel, 20 January 1943
129, 72 and 611 Squadrons
Theatre: Northern Europe
10 and 1 shared victories
(The picture shows Armstrong centre, with S/L G Slater and G/C A G Malan (34)

Dick
Flight Lieutenant Richard Joseph Audet
DFC*
From Lethbridge, Alberta, Canada, born 13 March 1922.
KIA, Coesfeld, Germany, 3 March 1945
411 RCAF Squadron
Theatre: France and Germany
10 and 1 shared victories

Nicky
Wing Commander Andrew William Barr
MC DFC*
From Melbourne Australia, born Wellington, New Zealand, 10 December 1915.
Died 12 June 2006
3 RAAF Squadron
Theatre: North Africa
11 victories

Alfie
Wing Commander Alfred William Alexander Bayne
DFC
Died 28 May 1963
17, 30 and 136 Squadrons
Theatres: BofB, Ceylon, Burma
7 and 4 shared victories

Birk
Colonel Kaj Birksted
DSO OBE DFC, Norwegian War Cross with Swords
From Denmark, but born 3 March 1915, Boston, USA. Died London, England, 23 January 1996
331 Norwegian Squadron, 132 Norwegian Wing
Theatre: Northern Europe
10 and 1 shared victories

Mike
Squadron Leader Michael Christopher Bindloss Boddington
DFC DFM
From Hawkshead, Lancashire. Died in New Guinea, 22 February 1977
234, 118, 19 and 242 Squadrons
Theatres: BofB, Northern Europe, Tunisia, Sicily and Italy
10 and 1 shared victories

Bogle
Flight Lieutenant Crelin Arthur Walford Bodie
DFC
Born Kirton, Suffolk, 1920. KIFA Eglinton, County Antrim, 24 February 1942
66, 310 Czech and 152 Squadrons
Theatres: BofB, Northern Europe
5 and 6 shared victories

Andy
Colonel Andrew Christiaan Bosman
DSO DFC
Born Bloemhof, Transvaal, SA, 16 May 1917. KIFA Khartoum, 17 April 1947
4 and 2 SAAF Squadrons, 7 SAAF Wing
Theatres: North Africa, Italy
8 and 3 shared victories

Flight Lieutenant Neville Bowker
DFC
From Orange Free State, SA, born in 1918. Died in road accident post war.
112 Squadron
Theatre: North Africa
10 and 1 shared victories
(The picture shows Bowker far right; left and centre are P H Humphreys (3) and FO J F Soden(4))

Les
Flying Officer Leslie Redford Clisby
DFC
Born in McLaren Vale, South Australia, 26 June 1914. KIA, France, 15 May 1940
1 Squadron
Theatre: France
8 and 3 shared victories

Flight Lieutenant Pierre Henri Clostermann
DFC* Ld'H, CdG
Born Curitiba, Brazil, 28 February 1921. Died Pyranees, 22 March 2006
341 (FF) Squadron, 602, 274, 56 and 3 Squadrons
Theatres: Northern Europe, France and Germany
11 victories*

Darkie
Squadron Leader Arthur Victor Clowes
DFC DFM
Born in New Sawley, Derbyshire. Died 7 December 1949, Cambridgeshire.
1, 79, 601 and 94 Squadrons
Theatres: France, North Africa
10 and 1 shared victories

Johnnie
Squadron Leader John Reynolds Cock
DFC
From Grange, South Australia, born 3 March 1918. Died 29 August 1988
87 Squadron
Theatres: France, BofB
10 and 1 shared victories

Dickie
Lieutenant-Commander Richard John Cork
DSO DSC (DFC*)
Born nr Brentford, London, 4 April 1917. KIFA, Ceylon, 14 April 1944
242 Squadron RAF, 880 Squadron FAA, 15 Wing FAA
Theatres: BofB, Mediterranean, Indian Ocean
9 and 2 shared victories
(*RAF awarded the DFC, the Navy replaced it with the DSC)

Squadron Leader Graham James Cox
DSO DFC*
Born Sparkhill, Birmingham, 1919. KIFA Canada, post war.
152, 43, 229 and 92 Squadrons
Theatres: BofB, Northern Europe, Malta, Sicily and Italy
8 and 3 shared victories

Squadron Leader Charles Arbuthnot Crombie
DSO DFC
From Warwick, Queensland, born 16 March 1914.
DoI, aircraft accident, Australia, 26 August 1945
89 and 176 Squadrons
Theatres: Night Fighter - North Africa, Malta, Sicily, India
11 victories
(Nav/Rad F/Lt Raymond Christopher Moss DFC)

Bill
Sergeant William Lawrence Dymond
DFM
Born Twickenham, Middlesex, 11 November 1917. KIA 2 September 1940
111 Squadron
Theatre: BofB
10 and 1 shared victories

Shag
Squadron Leader Alan Francis Eckford
DFC
From Thame, Oxfordshire. Died 6 December 1990
32, 242, 253 and 154 Squadrons
Theatres: France, BofB, Northern Europe, North Africa
8 and 3 shared victories

Mike
Flying Officer Henry Michael Ferris
DFC
From Lea, East London, born 1 August 1917. KIA 16 August 1940
111 Squadron
Theatre: BofB
9 and 2 shared victories

Geoff
Flying Officer Geoffrey Bryson Fisken
DFC
Born Gisborne, New Zealand, 17 February 1918
243, 453 RAAF and 14 RNZAF Squadrons
Theatres: Singapore, Solomons
11 victories

Gabby
Group Captain Aleksander Klemens Gabszewicz
DSO DFC Virtuti Militari (Gold and Silver), Cross of Valor***,
Dutch Order of Orange Nassau, CdG(Fr)
Born Szawle, Kowno, Poland, 6 December 1911. Died Hanley Swan, Worcs, 10 October 1983
114 Esk, GCIII/10, 316 Polish Squadron, 2 and 1 Polish Wings, 131 Wing
Theatres: Poland, France, Northern Europe, France and Germany
8 and 3 shared victories

Mike
Flight Lieutenant Michael John Gloster
DFC*
From Birmingham, born 1920.
255 and 219 Squadrons
Theatres: Night Fighter – North Africa, Normandy
11 victories
(Nav/Rad PO James Frederick Oswald DFC)

Doug
Major Douglas William Golding
DFC
Born Durban, South Africa, 9 April 1919
4 SAAF Squadron
Theatre: North Africa
8 and 3 shared victories

Don
Squadron Leader Donald Campbell Gordon
DFC*
Born Edmonton, Canada, 25 February 1920. Died Montreal, 26 June 1949
274, 601, 417 RCAF, 442 RCAF, 411 RCAF and 402 RCAF Squadrons
Theatres: North Africa, Italy, Germany
9 and 2 shared victories

Paddy

Group Captain Charles Patrick Green

DSO DFC DFC(US), Soviet Order of Patriotic War 1st Class

Born 30 March 1914. Died May 1999

92 Squadron, 421 Flight/91 and 600 Squadron

Theatres: Northern Europe, Night Fighter North Africa, Sicily & Italy

11 victories

(Nav/Rad F/O Reginald Joseph Gillies DFC*)

Captain Helmer Gustav Einer Grundt Spang

DFC*

Norwegian, born 7 June 1920. Died 10 August 1983

331 Norwegian Squadron

Theatres: Northern Europe, France & Germany

10 and 1 shared victories

Ronnie
Squadron Leader Ronald Fairfax Hamlyn
AFC DFM
Born Harrogate, N Yorkshire, 26 February 1914. Died April 1991
610 and 242 Squadrons
Theatre: BofB, Northern Europe
10 and 1 shared victories

Des
Flight Lieutenant Desmond Ibbotson
DFC*
Born Harewood, Leeds, 25 October 1915. KIFA Castel Nuovo, Italy, 19 November 1944
54, 112 and 601 Squadrons
Theatres: Northern Europe, North Africa, Italy
11 victories

Jamie
Flight Lieutenant George Esmond Jameson
DSO DFC
Born Rotherham, New Zealand, 20 November 1921
125 and 488 RNZAF Squadrons
Theatres: Night Home Defence, Normandy
11 victories
(Nav/Rad was F/Lt Arthur Norman Crookes DFC** RAF)
(Jameson left, Crookes on right)

Bob
Squadron Leader Robert Allan Kipp
DSO DFC*
Born Kamloops, BC, Canada, 12 October 1919. KIFA St Hubert, Canada, 25 July 1949
418 RCAF Squadron, Fighter Experimental Flight
Theatres: Intruder – Northern Europe and Germany
10 and 1 shared victories
(His Nav. was F/O Peter Huletsky DFC* RCAF)

Wing Commander John Hugh Lapsley
OBE DFC
Born Dacca, India, 24 September 1916. Died November 1995
80 and 274 Squadrons, 125 Wing
Theatres: North Africa, Normandy
11 victories

Dickie
Flight Lieutenant Richard Hugh Anthony Lee
DSO DFC
Born 12 May 1917, Curzon Hotel, Mayfair, London. KIA 18 August 1940
85 Squadron
Theatres: France, BofB
9 and 2 shared victories

Mickey
Flying Officer Michal Miroslav Maciejowski
DFC DFM, Virtuti Militari, Cross of Valor***
Born Poland, 29 October 1913. Died Winnipeg, Canada, 26 April 2001
111, 249, 317 Polish and 316 Polish Squadrons
Theatres: France, BofB, Northern Europe
10 and 1 shared victories

Boy
Flight Lieutenant Eric Simcox Marrs
DFC
Born Dover, 9 July 1921. KIA Brest, 24 July 1941
152 Squadron
Theatres: BofB, Northern Europe
6 and 5 shared victories

Red
Colonel Carroll Warren McColpin
DFC(Br), US Air Medals(7)
Born Buffalo, New York, 15 November 1914
71 and 133 (Eagle) Squadrons, US 336th FS, 404th Fighter Group
Theatre: Northern Europe
11 victories
(8 with RAF)

Andy
Flying Officer Wilfred Handel Miller
DFC*
Born North Wales, 27 September 1921. Died Bangor N.I., August 2000
125 and 169 Squadrons
Theatres: Night Home Defence, Night Bomber Support Germany
11 victories
(His Nav/Rad was F/O Frederick Charles Bone DFC*)

Bill
Pilot Officer William Henry Millington
DFC
Born in England, c.1917. KIA 30 October 1940
79 and 249 Squadrons
Theatre: BofB
9 and 2 shared victories

Mitch
Squadron Leader John Davidson Mitchner
DFC* Netherlands Flying Cross
Born Saskatoon, Sask, Canada, 3 July 1914. Died Penticton, BC, 8 December 1964
402, 421 and 416 RCAF Squadrons
Theatres: Northern Europe, Germany
10 and 1 shared victories

Boy
Squadron Leader Peter William Olbert Mould
DFC*
From Hallaton, Rutland (Leics) c.1917. KIA Malta, 1 October 1941
1, 261 and 185 Squadrons
Theatres: France, Malta
8 and 3 shared victories

Garry
Flight Lieutenant Gareth Leofric Nowell
DFM*
Born Handforth, Cheshire, 16 August 1912. Died Heathfield, Sussex, c.2000
87, 32 and 124 Squadrons
Theatres: France, Northern Europe
10 and 1 shared victories

Charles
Flight Lieutenant George Charles Calder Palliser
DFC
Born Cleveland, N Yorkshire, 11 January 1919
249 and 605 Squadrons
Theatres: BofB, Northern Europe, Malta
4 and 7 shared victories

Pilot Officer Nigel Manfred Park
DFM
Born Gisborne, New Zealand, 6 March 1921. KIA Malta, 25 October 1942
126 Squadron
Theatre: Malta
10 and 1 shared victories

Flying Officer Adolf Pietrasiak
DFM, Virtuti Militari, Cross of Valor
Born Poland. 17 November 1916. KIFA Channel, 29 November 1943
ECD Bourges, 92, 308 and 317 Polish Squadrons
Theatres: France, Northern Europe
7 and 4 shared victories

Paul
Wing Commander Paul Henry Mills Richey
DFC* Cdg(Fr), CdG(Bel),
Born Chelsea, London, 7 May 1916. Died 23 February 1989
1 and 609 Squadrons, 189 Wing
Theatres: France, Northern Europe, Burma
10 and 1 shared victories

Sammy
Flight Lieutenant Charles James Samouelle
DFC*
Born Islington, London, 2 February 1920. Died March 1997
92, 41 and 130 Squadrons
Theatres: North Africa, Germany
10 and 1 shared victories

Bill
Flight Lieutenant Wilfred Malcolm Skinner
DFM
Born Gloucester. Died 26 June 2003
74 Squadron
Theatres; BofB, Northern Europe
8 and 3 shared victories
(To the front and right is F/L J C Mungo-Park (13))

Flight Lieutenant Harry Steere
DFC DFM
From Wallasey, Cheshire, born c.1914. KIA St Erblon, France, 9 June 1944.
19 Squadron
Theatre: BofB, Bomber Command
6 and 5 shared victories

Sneezy
Wing Commander Henryk Szczesny
Born Ruszkowo, Poland, 27 March 1909. Died London, England, 25 July 1996
DFC, Virtuti Militari (Silver), Cross of Valor**
Deblin Group, 74, 302 and 317 Polish Squadrons, Northolt Wing
Theatres: Poland, BofB, Northern Europe
8 and 3 shared victories

Group Captain Peter Wooldridge Townsend
DSO DFC*
Born Rangoon, Burma, 22 November 1914. Died France, 20 June 1995
43, 85, 605 Squadrons
Theatres: BofB, Night Home Defence
9 and 2 shared victories

Flight Lieutenant Hamilton Charles Upton
DFC
Born Manchester, England. Died 1965
43 and 607 Squadrons
Theatre: BofB
10 and 1 shared victories

Jerry
Squadron Leader Derrick Fitzgerald Westenra
DFC*
Born Christchurch, New Zealand, 29 April 1918. Died September 1999
112, 601 and 65 Squadrons
Theatres: Greece, North Africa, Tunisia, Sicily and Italy, Normandy
8 and 3 shared victories

Wing Commander George Herbert Westlake
DSO DFC
Born Rangoon, Burma, 21 April 1918. Died 18 January 2006
213 and 80 Squadrons, 239 Wing
Theatres: Northern Europe, Syria, Cyprus, North Africa, Italy
9 and 2 shared victories

Flight Lieutenant Alan Frederick Aikman
DFC*
Born Toronto, Canada, 5 March 1919. Deceased
134 and 154
Theatres: Northern Europe, Tunisia, Sicily
8 and 2 shared victories

Jim
Wing Commander James Michel Bazin
DSO DFC
Born Kashmir, India, 1913. Died in January 1985
607 Squadron
Theatres: France, BofB, Bomber Command
8 and 2 shared victories

Victor
Group Captain Francis Victor Beamish
DSO* DFC AFC
Born Dunmanway, County Cork, Eire, 27 September 1903. KIA Channel, 28 March 1942
151 Squadron, RAF Northolt, North Weald Wing
Theatres: BofB, Northern Europe
10 victories

Bee
Wing Commander Roland Prosper Beamont
DSO* DFC* DFC(US),
Born Enfield, N London, 10 August 1920. Died 19 November 2001
87, 56 and 609, 150 Wing
Theatres: France, BofB, Northern Europe, Normandy
9 and 1 shared victories

Ben
Wing Commander James Ghillies Benson
DSO DFC*
Born Tufnell Park, N London, 17 July 1914. Died 1987
141 and 157 Squadrons
Theatres: Night Home Defence, Intruder – France and Germany
10 victories
(His main Nav/Rad was S/Ldr Lewis Brandon DSO DFC*)
(Benson left, Brandon on the right)

The Bish
Group Captain John Derek Bisdee
OBE DFC
Born Weston-Super-Mare, Somerset, 20 November 1915. Died Colchester, October 2000
609 and 601 Squadrons
Theatres: BofB, Northern Europe, Malta, North Africa, Italy
8 and 2 shared victories

Archie
Wing Commander Archibald Douglas McNeill Boyd
DSO DFC
Born 20 June 1918, Sheffield.
600 and 219 Squadrons
Theatres: Home Night Defence, Night Fighting – Mediterranean
10 victories
(His Nav/Rad was F/Lt Alexander Jospeh Glegg DFC* died 1992)
(Glegg left, Boyd on the right)

Paul
Flight Lieutenant Virgil Paul Brennan
DFC DFM
Born Warwick, Queensland, Australia, 6 March 1920. KIFA, Garbutt, Queensland 13 June 1943
249 Squadron, 79 RAAF Squadron
Theatre: Malta
10 victories

Flight Lieutenant Stanislaw Brzeski
DFC, Virtuti Militari, Cross of Valor****
Born Lipniki, Poland, 21 April 1918. Died 3 December 1972
152 Esk, GCII/1, 249, 317 and 302 (Polish) Squadrons
Theatres: Poland, France, Northern Europe
7 and 3 shared victories

Werner
Lieutenant-Colonel Werner Hosewinckel Christie
Born Vang, Norway, 13 December 1917. Died 28 December 2004
DSO DFC, Norwegian War Cross & Swords, St Olav's Medal with Oak Leaves,
Knight's Cross of the Swedish Sword Order
332 and 234 Squadrons, Hunsdon Wing
Theaters: Northern Europe, Germany
9 and 1 shared victories

Billy
Group Captain William Pancoast Clyde
DFC
British born, living in Mexico
601 Squadron
Theatre: BofB
9 and 1 shared victories

Ern
Flight Lieutenant Edward Ernest Coate
DFC*
Born Lake Entrance, Victoria, Australia, 13 August 1908
272 Squadron
Theatres: Egypt and Mediterranean
9 and 1 shared victories

Flying Officer Carl Raymond Davis
DFC
American, born in South Africa, c.1911. KIA 6 September 1940
601 Squadron
Theatre: BofB
9 and 1 shared victories

Pilot Officer Charles Trevor Davis
DFC
From Cardiff, South Wales, born 8 June 1920. KIFA 26 March 1941
238 Squadron
Theatre: BofB
4 and 6 shared victories
(NO PHOTO AVAILABLE)

Ken
Major Kenneth Weekes Driver
DFC
Born Brooklyn, Pretoria, SA, 3 April 1918.
KIFA nr. Wotton Under Edge, England, 3 February 1947
1 SAAF Squadron, 274 Squadron
Theatres: Sudan, Eritrea, Crete, North Africa
10 victories

Cocky
Group Captain Hugh Spencer Lisle Dundas
DSO* DFC
Born nr. Doncaster, W Yorkshire, 22 July 1920. Died 11 July 1995
616 and 56 Squadrons, Duxford, 324 and 244 Wings
Theatres: BofB, Northern Europe, Sicily and Italy
4 and 6 shared victories

Crash
Commander Charles Les Glandore Evans
DSO DSC
Born 2 August 1908. Died Athens, Greece, 27 December 1981
803, 806 FAA Squadrons
Theatres: North Sea, Mediterranean, Pacific
2 and 8 shared victories

Tony
Wing Commander Anthony Eyre
DFC
Born Lowestoft, Suffolk, 1918. KIFA St Athan, 16 February 1946
615 Squadron, North Weald Wing
Theatres: France, BofB, Northern Europe
8 and 2 shared victories

Ox
Flying Officer Miroslaw Feric
DFC, Virtuti Militari, Cross of Valor**
Born Travnik, Yugoslavia, 17 June 1915. KIFA Northolt, 14 February 1942
111 Esk, 303 Polish Squadron
Theatres: Poland, BofB, Northern Europe
8 and 2 shared victories

Joe
Wing Commander Joseph Frederick Fraser
DFC
Born Colombo, Ceylon, 11 February 1915. Died jeep accident Ankara, Turkey, 11 August 1946
112 Squadron
Theatres: North Africa, Greece
9 and 1 shared victories

Jimmie
Commander Richard Exton Gardner
OBE DSC
Died 26 March 1999
242 Squadron RAF, 807 and 889 FAA Squadrons
Theatres: BofB, Mediterranean, Western Desert
6 and 4 shared victories
(Dickie Cork (11) is on the left, Gardner on the right)

Geoff
Wing Commander Geoffrey William Garton
DSO DFC
Born Grantham, Lincolnshire, 3 October 1915. Died November 1976
73, 250, 112 and 87 Squadrons
Theatres: France, BofB, North Africa, Italy
7 and 3 shared victories

Jumbo
Flight Lieutenant George Eric Clifford Genders
DFM
Born Oldham, Lancashire, 15 February 1920. KIFA 1 May 1950
33 Squadron, 103 MU
Theatres: Greece, North Africa, Egypt
8 and 2 shared victories

Goose
Flying Officer Leslie Cyril Gosling
DFC*
From Battleford, Sask., Canada, born 5 October 1920. KIA Italy, 19 July 1943
222 and 229 Squadrons
Theatres: Northern Europe, Malta/Tunisia, Sicily and Italy
9 and 1 shared victories

Jumbo
Wing Commander Edward John Gracie
DFC
Born Acton, West London, 21 September 1911. KIA Germany, 15 February 1944
56, 23, 126 and 169 Squadrons
Theatres: BofB, Northern Europe, Malta, Bomber Command/Germany
7 and 3 shared victories

Major Martin Yngvar Gran
DFC**
From Norway, born 13 September 1917. Died 16 May 2004
331 RNAF Squadron
Theatre: Northern Europe, France and Germany
8 and 2 shared victories

Flight Lieutenant Glyn Griffiths
DFM
Born Llundudno, N Wales, 1918. Died Surrey, 1983
17 and 4 Squadrons
Theatres: BofB, Northern Europe
5 and 5 shared victories

Frankie
Squadron Leader Frank Jonathan Howell
DFC*
Born Golders Green NW London, 25 January 1912. KOAS Odiham, 9 May 1948
609, 118 and 243 Squadrons
Theatres: BofB, Northern Europe, Singapore
7 and 3 shared victories

Squadron Leader Philip Algernon Hunter
DSO
From Frimley, Surrey, born 1913. KIA 24 August 1940
264 Squadron
Theatre: Dunkirk/BofB
9 and 1 shared victories
(His Air Gunner was Sergeant Frederick Harry King DFM – KIA 24 August 1940)
(Hunter is at top, King at bottom)

Donald
Squadron Leader Aeneas Ranald Donald MacDonnell
DFC
A Scot, born Baku, Russia, 15 November 1913. Died 6 June 1999
64 Squadron
Theatres: BofB, Northern Europe
9 and 1 shared victories

Mac
Squadron Leader John Noble Mackenzie
DFC
Born Goodwood, Otago, NZ, 11 August 1914. Died NZ, 28 March 1993
41, 488 (NZ) and 64 Squadrons
Theatres: BofB, Singapore, Normandy
8 and 2 shared victories

Squadron Leader Miloslav Jan Mansfeld
DSO DFC, Czech War Cross
Born Dalovice, Czechoslovakia, 14 December 1912. Died Hampstead, North London, 22 October 1991
111 and 68 Squadrons
Theatres: Day Home Defence, Night Home Defence
8 and 2 shared victories
(Nav/Rad F/L S A Janacek DFC DFM 1914-73)

Pat
Group Captain Patrick Edward Meagher
DSO DFC
Born Haulbowline, County Cork, Eire, in 1910
41, 602 and 211 Squadrons, 169 Wing
Theatres: Northern Europe, Burma
10 victories

Black
Wing Commander James Storrs Morton
DFC*
Born Blackheath, S London, 24 April 1916. Died 1982
603, 54 and 219 Squadrons
Theatres: BofB, Night Home Defence, Night Fighter Tunisia
6 and 4 shared victories

Bennie
Lieutenant-Colonel Malcolm Stephen Osler
DFC*
Born Benoni, South Africa, 7 March 1919. Died Jo'burg, 22 September 1971
1 SAAF, 145 and 601 Squadrons
Theatres: North Africa, Italy
9 and 1 shared victories

Squadron Leader John Ernest Proctor
DFC
Born 15 July 1913. Died in South Africa, early 1990s
501, 32, 33 and 352 (Yugoslav) Squadrons
Theatres: France, BofB, North Africa, Italy
9 and 1 shared victories

Roddy
Wing Commander Roderick Malachi Seaborne Rayner
DFC
Born 6 January 1918. Died 28 December 1982
87 Squadron
Theatres: France, BofB
8 and 2 shared victories

Jasper
Wing Commander James Alfred Avory Read
DFC*
Born 11 August 1911. Died 12 December 1979
89, 219 Gp HQ, 46 and 108 Squadrons
Theatres: Night Fighter Egypt, Sicily and Italy
10 victories
(NO PHOTO AVAILABLE)

John
Group Captain John William Charles Simpson
DFC*
Born Ramsey St Mary, Huntingdonshire, 1913. Died 12 August 1949
43 and 245 Squadrons
Theatres: BofB, Home Defence
9 and 1 shared victories

Wing Commander Gordon Leonard Sinclair
DFC, Czech War Cross
Born Eastbourne, Sussex, 15 August 1916. Died 26 June 2005
19, 310 (Czech) and 56 Squadrons
Theatres: BofB, Northern Europe
10 victories

Squadron Leader Otto Smik
DFC*
Born 20 January 1922, Borzomi, Russia. KIA Holland, 28 November 1944
122, 222, 310 (Czech) and 127 Squadrons
Theatres: Northern Europe, Normandy, France and Germany
8 and 2 shared victories

Bob
Squadron Leader Robert Lawrence Spurdle
DFC*
Born Wanganui, New Zealand, 3 March 1918. Died in NZ, 5 March 1994
74, 91 Squadrons, 16 RNZAF Squadron, 130 and 80 Squadrons
Theatres: Northern Europe, Solomons, France and Germany
10 victories

Flight Lieutenant Josef Stehlik
Born Pikarec, Czechoslovakia, 23 March 1915. Died Slavicin, 30 May 1991
GCIII/3, 312 Czech Squadron, 1 Czech Regt(USSR)
Theatres: France, BofB, Northern Europe, Russia
3 and 7 shared victories
(2 shared with RAF)

Flight Lieutenant Leslie Stephenson
DFC*
Born Langley Moor, County Durham, in 1921
141, 153 and 219 Squadrons
Theatres: Night Fighter North Africa, France and Germany
10 victories
(His Nav/Rad was Flying Officer George Arthur Hall DFC*)
(Stephenson left, Hall on the right)

Bob
Lieutenant Robert Henry Talbot
Born Boksburg, South Africa, 27 June 1916. KIA 3 June 1941
274 and 1 SAAF Squadrons
Theatres: Egypt/Libya, Crete, North Africa
9 and 1 shared victories

Jack
Squadron Leader John Ronald Urwin-Mann
DSO DFC*
British, born Vancouver, Canada, 30 July 1920, lived in Hove, Sussex.
Died Sussex, UK, 7 March 1999
238, 80 and 126 Squadrons
BofB, North Africa, Sicily
8 and 2 shared victories

Vass
Flying Officer Basilios Michael Vassiliades
DFC DFM
Born Chios, Greece. KIA 25 March 1945
19 and 3 Squadrons
Theatres: Northern Europe, Normandy, France and Germany
8 and 2 shared victories

Wimpy
Squadron Leader Trevor Sidney Wade
DFC AFC
Born 1920. KIFA Ringmer, Sussex, 3 April 1951
92, 123 and 602 Squadrons
Theatres: BofB, Northern Europe
6 and 4 shared victories

Wing Commander James Elmslie Walker
DFC**
Born Claresholm, Alberta, Canada, 4 April 1919. DoI/FA Tangmere, 26 April 1944
81 and 243 Squadrons, 127 and 126 Airfields
Theatres: N Russia, Northern Europe, Tunisia
9 and 1 shared victories

Babe
Squadron Leader William Michael Whitamore
DFC
Born 26 July 1922. KIA Burma, 17 March 1944
66, 92, 112, 601 and 81 Squadrons
Theatres: Northern Europe, North Africa, Sicily/Italy, Burma
9 and 1 shared victories

Pete
Wing Commander Peter Reginald Whalley Wickham
DSO DFC*, Silver Star(US)
Born Nairobi, Kenya, 26 March 1918. Died 29 April 1970
112, 33, 111, 122 Squadrons, 122 and Peterhead Wings
Theatres: North Africa, Greece, Northern Europe
10 victories

Wilkie
Wing Commander Royce Clifford Wilkinson
OBE DFM* CdG(Fr)
Born Mexborough, Yorkshire, 26 November 1913. Died Sheppey, 13 January 1990
3, 71 and 1 Squadrons
Theatres: France, Northern Europe
7 and 3 shared victories

Squadron Leader John Ellis Willson
DFC*
Born Bowes Park, London, 13 September 1912. KIA Algiers, 27 August 1943
219 and 153 Squadrons
Theatres: Night Home Defence, Night Fighter North Africa
10 victories
(NO PHOTO AVAILABLE)

To find the picture and detail, take the number in the third column and locate the pilot in the relevant section. e.g.: to find A.F. Aikman, look in the section dealing with aces with 10 victories.

Aikman, FL A F	8	2	10
Aitken, GC The Hon J W M	14	1	15
Allan, WC J W	14	-	14
Allard, FL G	16	5	21
Armstrong, SL H T	10	1	11
Atkinson, PO H D	9	3	12
Audet, FL R J	10	1	11
Bader, GC D R S	20	4	24
Baldwin, GC J R	15	1	16
Barr, WC A W	11	-	11
Bartley, SL A C	12	1	13
Barton, WC R A	10	4	14
Bayne, WC A W A	7	4	11
Bazin, WC J M	8	2	10
Beamish, GC F V	9	1	10
Beamont, WC R P	9	1	10
Bennions, SL G H	12	-	12
Benson, WC J G	10	-	10
Berry, WC R	14	10	24
Beurling, FL G F	31	1	32
Birksted, Col K	10	1	11
Bisdee, GC J D	8	2	10
Blake, WC M V	10	3	13
Blakeslee, Col D J M	14	1	15
Boddington, SL M C B	10	1	11
Bodie, FL C A W	5	6	11
Bosman, Col A C	8	3	11
Bowker, FL N	10	1	11
Boyd, WC A D McN	10	-	10
Boyd, GC A H	15	3	18
Boyd, GC R F	14	7	21
Braham, WC J R D	29	-	29
Brennan, FL V P	10	-	10
Broadhurst, AVM H	13	-	13
Brothers, WC P M	16	-	16
Brown, WC M H	15	4	19
Brzeski, FL S	7	3	10
Buchanan, WC J K	10	3	13
Burbridge, WC B A	21	-	21
Caldwell, WC C R	26	4	30
Carbury, FL B J G	15	2	17
Carey, GC F R	25	3	28
Casbolt, PO C E	13	1	14
Charles, WC E F J	15	1	16
Checketts, WC J M	14	-	14*

Christie, Lt-Col W H	9	1	10
Clisby, FO L R	8	3	11
Clostermann, FL P H	11	-	11*
Clouston, WC W G	9	3	12
Clowes, SL A V	10	1	11
Clyde, GC W P	9	1	10
Coate, FL E E	9	1	10
Cock, SL J R	10	1	11
Connors, FL S D P	12	-	12
Cooke, FL N G	9	3	12
Cooper-Slipper, SL T P M	9	3	12
Cork, Lt-Cdr R J	9	2	11
Cottingham, FO L	11	1	12
Cox, SL G J	8	3	11
Crawford-Compton, WC W V	21	1	22
Crew, WC E D	12	1	13
Crombie, SL C A	11	-	11
Crossley, WC M N	20	2	22
Cullen, FL R N	15	1	16
Cunningham, GC J	20	-	20
Curchin, FL J	8	5	13
Currant, WC C F	10	5	15
Czernin, SL Count M B	13	6	19
Dalton-Morgan, GC T F	14	3	17
Daniel, SL S W	16	1	17
David, GC W D	15	2	17
Davis, FO C R	9	1	10
Davis, PO C T	4	6	10
Davison, FL M M	12	-	12
De Hemricourt de Grunne, PO R G C	11	1	12
De La Poype, Capt R	7	9	16
Deere, WC A C	18	1	19
Demozay, WC J-F	18	-	18
Dodds, Sgt J	13	-	13
Doe, SL R F T	14	2	16
Doleman, SL R D	10	2	12
Downing, FL A B	12	-	12
Drake, GC B	23	3	26
Driver, Maj K W	10	-	10
Duke, SL N F	27	2	29
Duncan Smith, GC W G G	17	2	19
Dundas, GC H S L	4	6	10
Dundas, FL J C	12	4	16
Dutton, WC R G	13	6	19
Dymond, Sgt W L	10	1	11
Eckford, SL A F	8	3	11*
Edge, GC G R	18	2	20
Edwards, WC J F	15	3	18
Ellis, WC J	13	2	15
Evans, Cdr C L G	2	8	10
Eyre, WC A	8	2	10

Fairbanks, SL D C	12	1	13
Feric, FO M	9	1	10
Ferriss, FO H M	9	2	11
Finucane, WC B E F	26	6	32
Fisken, FO G B	11	-	11
Fokes, SL R H	9	4	13
Franklin, PO W H	13	3	16
Frantisek, Sgt J	17	-	17
Fraser, WC J F	9	1	10
Freeborn, WC J C	12	1	13
Frost, Maj J E	14	2	16
Fumerton, WC R C	14	-	14
Gabszewicz, GC A K	8	3	11
Gardner, Cdr R E	6	4	10
Garton, WC G W	7	3	10
Gaze, SL F A O	11	3	14
Genders, FL G E C	8	2	10*
Gentile, Capt D S	21	2	23
Gibbes, WC R H M	10	2	12
Gibson, SL J A A	12	1	13
Gilroy, GC G K	14	11	25
Gladych, Maj B M	17	-	17
Gleed, WC I R	13	3	16
Gloster, FL M J	11	-	11
Golding, Maj D W	8	3	11
Goldsmith, SL A P	16	1	17
Goodman, FO G E	10	6	16
Gordon, SL D C	9	2	11
Gosling, FO L C	9	1	10
Gracie, WC E J	7	3	10
Gran, Maj M Y	8	2	10
Gray, WC C F	27	2	29
Green, GC C P	11	-	11
Green, WC W P	14	-	14
Grier, SL T	8	4	12
Griffiths, FL G	5	5	10
Grundt-Spang, Capt H G E	10	1	11
Haines, FO L A	8	4	12
Hallowes, WC H J L	17	2	19
Hamlyn, SL R F	10	1	11
Hanbury, SL O V	10	2	12
Hanks, GC P P	11	4	15
Harries, WC R H	15	3	18
Hay, Lt-Col R C	4	9	13
Heglund, Capt S	15	1	16
Hesselyn, FL R B	18	1	19*
Hewitt, FL E W F	16	-	16
Higginson, FL F W	12	-	12
Hill, SL G U	10	8	18
Hodgkinson, FL A J	12	-	12

Hogg, Sub-Lt G A	4	8	12
Horbaczewski, SL E	16	1	17
Houle, SL A U	12	1	13
Howell, SL F J	7	3	10
Howes, Sgt H N	11	1	12
Hughes, WC F D	18	1	19
Hughes, FL P C	14	3	17
Hugo, GC P H	17	3	20
Hunter, SL P A	9	1	10
Hussey, FL R J H	9	5	14
Ibbotson, FL D	11	-	11
Ingram, SL M R B	8	6	14
Jameson, FL G E	11	-	11
Johnson, WC J E	34	7	41
Johnston, WC G R A McG	10	2	12
Kain, FL E J	16	-	16
Keefer, WC G C	12	-	12
Kennedy, SL I F	10	5	15
Kent, GC J A	12	-	12
Kilmartin, WC J I	10	2	12
Kingaby, WC D E	21	2	23
Kingcome, GC C B F	9	3	12
Kipp, SL R A	10	1	11
Klersy, SL W T	14	1	15
Kuttelwascher, FL K M	18	2	20
Lacey, SL J H	28	-	28
Lapsley, WC J H	11	-	11
Laubman, SL D C	14	2	16
Lee, FL R H A	9	2	11
LeRoux, SL J J	18	-	18
Lewis, SL A G	16	-	16
Littolf, Capt A	6	8	14
Llewellyn, FL R T	13	1	14
Lock, FL E S	26	-	26
Lovell, WC A D J	16	6	22
Lynch, SL J J	10	7	17
MacDonnell, SL A R D	9	1	10
Maciejowski, FO M M	10	1	11
MacKay, FL J	11	2	13
MacKenzie, SL J N	8	2	10
MacKenzie, FL K W	10	3	13
Mackie, WC E D	20	3	23
MacLachlan, SL J A F	16	1	17
Maguire, FL W I H	13	-	13
Malan, GC A G	27	7	34
Mansfeld, SL M J	8	2	10
Marrs, FL E S	6	5	11
Marshall, FL A E	16	2	18
Mason, SL E M	15	2	17
Mayers, WC H C	11	1	12
McColpin, Col C W	11	-	11
McDowell, WC A	11	2	13
McElroy, SL J F	13	3	16
McKay, FL D A S	16	1	17
McKeller, SL A A	17	3	20
McKnight, FO W L	17	2	19
McLeod, SL H W	21	-	21
McMullen, WC D A P	17	5	22
McNair, WC R W	16	-	16
Meagher, GC P E	10	-	10
Miller, FO W H	11	-	11
Millington, PO W H	9	2	11
Milne, WC R M	14	1	15
Mitchner, SL J D	10	1	11
Mortimer-Rose, FL E B	9	4	13
Morton, WC J S	6	4	10
Mould, SL P W O	8	3	11
Mungo-Park, SL J C	11	2	13
Nash, PO P A	11	1	12
Neil, WC T F	12	4	16
Nowell, FL G L	10	1	11
O'Meara, SL J J	11	2	13
Orr, Lt-Cdr S G	7	7	14
Orton, SL N	17	-	17
Osler, Lt-Col M S	9	1	10
Owen, SL A J	15	-	15
Oxspring, WC R W	13	2	15
Page, WC A G	10	5	15
Palliser, FL G C C	4	7	11
Park, PO N M	10	1	11
Pattle, SL M T StJ	50	2	52
Perina, FO F	3	9	12
Pietrasiak, FO A	7	4	11
Pisarek, WC M	11	2	13
Plagis, WC J A	15	2	17
Proctor, SL J E	9	1	10
Rabagliati, WC A C	16	1	17
Rae, FO J D	11	2	13
Rankin, AC J	17	5	22
Rayner, WC R M S	8	2	10
Read, WC J A A	10	-	10
Reeves, WC N E	14	-	14
Richey, WC P H M	10	1	11
Riley, WC W	9	3	12
Robertson, FO F N	11	1	12
Robinson, WC M L	18	-	18
Rolls, FL W T E	17	1	18
Samouelle, FL CJ	10	1	11
Sanders, WC J G	15	1	16
Schade, FO P A	12	-	12
Scherf SL C C	13	1	14
Schrader, WC W E	11	2	13
Scoular, SL J E	14	3	17
Sewell, Lt-Cdr A J	6	7	13
Shepherd, SL J B	8	5	13
Shipard, FL M C	13	-	13
Simpson, GC J W C	9	1	10
Sinclair, WC G L	10	-	10
Sizer, WC W M	7	6	13
Skalski, WC S	18	3	21
Skinner, FL W H	8	3	11
Smik, SL O	8	2	10
Smith, SL R I A	13	1	14
Soper, SL F J	11	4	15
Spurdle, SL R L	10	-	10
Steere, FL H	6	5	11
Stehlik, Capt J	3	7	10
Stenborg, FL G	14	1	15
Stephen, WC H M	9	8	17
Stephens, WC M M	18	3	21
Stephenson, FL L	10	-	10
Stevens, FL R P	14	1	15
Stones, SL D W A	7	5	12
Storrar, WC J E	12	2	14
Szczesny, WC H	8	3	11
Talbot, Lt R H	9	1	10
Taylor, SL J S	13	2	15
Thorn, SL E R	12	1	13
Topham, WC J G	13	-	13
Townsend, GC P W	9	2	11
Truscott, SL K W	14	-	14
Tuck, WC R R S	27	2	29
Turkington, SL R W	9	3	12
Turnbull, FL J H	12	1	13
Turnbull, SL P StG B	12	-	12
Turner, GC P S	13	1	14
Unwin, FL G C	13	2	15
Upton, FL H C	10	1	11
Urbanowicz, WC W	18	-	18
Urwin-Mann, SL J R	8	2	10

Vale, SL W	30	3	33
Vasatko, WC A	4	10	14
Vassiliades, FO B M	8	2	10
Villa, SL J W	13	4	17
Waddy, WC J L	15	1	16
Wade, WC L C	23	2	25
Wade, SL T S	6	4	10
Walker, WC J E	9	1	10
Walmsley, SL H E	11	1	12
Weaver III, PO C	12	1	13
Webster, FL J T	11	2	13
Wedgwood, SL J H	10	3	13
Wells, WC E P	12	-	12
Westenra, SL D F	8	3	11
Westlake, WC G H	9	2	11
Whitamore, SL W M	9	1	10
White, FL H E	12	-	12
Whittle, SL R J C	11	3	14
Wickham, WC P R W	10	-	10
Wilkinson, WC R C	7	3	10
Willson, SL J E	10	-	10
Woods, WC E N	10	2	12
Woods-Scawen, FO P P	11	3	14
Woodward, WC V C	18	4	22
Wright, WC A R	11	3	14
Wykeham-Barnes, GC P G	14	3	17
Yarra, FL J W	12	-	12
Young, SL M H	7	6	13
Zumbach, SL J E L	12	2	14

*possibly more